AND ACTION!

DIRECTING DOCUMENTARIES IN THE SOCIAL STUDIES CLASSROOM

Kathy Swan and Mark Hofer

ROWMAN & LITTLEFIELD EDUCATION

A division of
ROWMAN & LITTLEFIELD
Lanham • Boulder • New York • Toronto • Plymouth, UK

KH

Published by Rowman & Littlefield Education
A division of Rowman & Littlefield
4501 Forbes Boulevard, Suite 200, Lanham, Maryland 20706
www.rowman.com

10 Thornbury Road, Plymouth PL6 7PP, United Kingdom

Copyright © 2014 by Kathy Swan and Mark Hofer

British Library Cataloguing in Publication Information Available

Library of Congress Cataloging-in-Publication Data

Swan, Kathy, 1969–
  And action! : directing documentaries in the social studies classroom / Kathy Swan and Mark Hofer.
    page cm
  Includes index.
  ISBN 978-1-4758-0147-7 (cloth : alk. paper) — ISBN 978-1-4758-0148-4 (pbk. : alk. paper) — ISBN 978-1-4758-0149-1 (electronic) 1. Social sciences—Study and teaching—Audio-visual aids. 2. Documentary films—Production and directing. 3. Video recordings—Production and directing. I. Hofer, Mark, 1972– II. Title.
  LB1584.S935 2014
  372.83—dc23   2013028534

∞™ The paper used in this publication meets the minimum requirements of American National Standard for Information Sciences—Permanence of Paper for Printed Library Materials, ANSI/NISO Z39.48-1992.

Printed in the United States of America

9/8/15

CONTENTS

FOREWORD

"Nobody works harder at learning than a curious kid."
> —Thomas Friedman, *The World is Flat*

In the recently published C3 Social Studies Framework, peaking students' interests and curiosities about the world are placed at the center of doing authentic social studies. As educators, it is our responsibility to provide opportunities for students to channel these interests into experiences that allow them to practice a variety of skills and dispositions that will prepare them for college, career, and most importantly, a productive and engaged civic life.

In this book, Kathy Swan and Mark Hofer make the case for student filmmaking as a mechanism to engage students in the exploration of compelling questions and the construction of complex answers. Additionally, they move beyond advocacy and do the hard work of teaching us how we equip students with the knowledge and skills to do documentary making well. By fusing together the research on social studies, technology, and film, and providing important resources to teachers, students can be empowered to do the ambitious work of student documentary making as part of the core social studies curriculum. As students creatively build evidence-based arguments and interpretations on important social issues and events, they are developing civic skills necessary to sustaining a vibrant democracy.

If you are an ambitious teacher looking for powerful ways to engage your students in the kind of authentic intellectual work that should be a part of any learning experience, *And Action! Directing Documentaries in the Social Studies Classroom* is an essential resource to help move you along on your professional journey.

Susan Griffin,
Executive Director of the
National Council for the Social Studies

PREFACE

And Action! Directing Documentaries in the Social Studies Classroom provides social studies teachers with the background knowledge, conceptual understanding, and tools necessary for guiding their students to create digital documentaries in the K–12 social studies classroom.

We have spent more than 10 years in classrooms working collaboratively with teachers to design and research classroom documentary projects. Recognizing the challenges of this kind of work, we have also partnered with filmmakers, historians, educational technologists, and classroom teachers with experience in leading documentary projects to develop a robust production process that closely mirrors the work of filmmakers.

With this book, we draw on all of these experiences to assist social studies educators to efficiently and effectively structure and assess documentary projects in ways that help students move away from "digital encyclopedia entries" toward a more authentic documentary approach that focuses on disciplined inquiry and the use of evidence-based arguments.

Although the potential for student-created documentaries is well established in the research literature, guiding students in the documentary process is no small challenge. Student documentary making is an intricate and layered learning process that requires pre-teaching of skills (e.g., argumentation and use of evidence) as well as a variety of scaffolds in the form of teacher feedback (e.g., formative and summative) throughout the filmmaking project. Current books on the market focus on the *potential of* and *enthusiasm for* digital storytelling. Although we agree that documentary making is worth doing, successful projects are dependent upon thoughtful construction and implementation and include an honest discussion of how projects can go wrong and, in our experience, have gone wrong.

We believe that our time in classrooms working out the inevitable pedagogical and technical challenges alongside teachers and studying student products across a range of social studies disciplines, grade levels, and contexts allows us to speak to teachers in encouraging but frank ways about the affordances and constraints of filmmaking in K–12 classrooms.

Why write a book about documentary making then? First, documentary making is a tool that social scientists use to communicate ideas and arguments across the social studies disciplines (e.g., Ken Burns's films; *An Inconvenient Truth*; *Food, Inc.*; *Inside Job*; *Waiting for Superman*). Thus, it is an authentic medium within the social studies disciplines. In fact, National History Day (NHD) has recently created a new documentary category for their annual history contest. Competitions like NHD provide creative opportunities for students, but there are few resources history teachers and students can access that will guide them in the process for the K–12 classroom.

The main objectives of this book are to (1) provide a rationale for student-created documentaries by summarizing the research to date on documentary making in the social studies classroom; (2) articulate a scaffolded production process composed of four distinct but fluid phases (research, treatment, storyboarding, production); (3) provide social studies educators with reproducible resources (e.g., rubrics, storyboards) to assist them in preparing for and facilitating the documentary-making process; and (4) anchor the process with helpful tips and advice from social studies teachers who have directed documentary projects in a variety of contexts, including different grade levels, subject matter (e.g., history, economics, civics, and geography), and technology infrastructure (e.g., a few computing stations, one-to-one access, one laptop, or a single computer).

ORGANIZATION OF THE BOOK

Chapter 1 provides a theoretical frame and rationale for engaging students in the process of creating documentary films. Rather than using technology as an add-on or embellishment to the learning experience, the production of classroom documentaries is a way to help students develop 21st-century skills while simultaneously addressing the College, Career and Civic Life (C3) Framework for Social Studies State Standards, Common Core State Standards for English Language Arts/Literacy in History/Social Science and Technical Subjects, and specific kinds of disciplinary thinking essential to the social studies.

In chapter 2, the reader is introduced to the notion of filmmaking as a powerful but challenging new medium within which students can share their understanding. Emphasis is placed on how the documentary medium can be used to encourage students to develop multimodal, evidence-based arguments in social studies courses—a particularly engaging form of authentic intellectual work (AIW). A brief overview of the four-phase documentary film production process that is the core of this book is then introduced. This chapter concludes with noting the importance of classroom and computer context and how these factors influence the creation of a documentary project.

The first phase of the documentary production process, research, is the focus of chapter 3. The importance of scaffolding student work in this phase is stressed throughout the chapter—by providing evocative questions to help students guide their research. Pragmatic suggestions for assisting students in finding relevant and appropriate research material, working with different forms of evidence and data, and documenting the source of their research materials are all covered in depth. The chapter concludes with a discussion of how to help students to articulate an evidence-based argument that will become the focus for their films.

Chapter 4 is structured around Phase 2 of the documentary process, the development of the documentary treatment. This chapter focuses on helping students to develop the "pitch" for their films—or the focus and synopsis of their films in a brief synopsis. The chapter then introduces the three-act narrative structure and helps students outline their stories in preparation for creating their storyboards.

In chapter 5, you will be introduced to the storyboarding phase. This chapter will help you to lead your students through the process of transitioning to the visual medium of filmmaking as they develop the blueprints for their final production phase. Specifically, the image rough cut process, scriptwriting, and the identification and application of visual and sound elements will be explained and explored.

Chapter 6 covers the final phase of the documentary creation process—production. In this chapter, a number of video editing options will be explored and guidance will be provided on selecting the most appropriate tool for your students to use in creating their films. The heart of this chapter is in the description of student roles and responsibilities in this final, critical phase of the work.

Discussion of the formative and summative assessment of student work throughout the four phases of the process is embedded throughout the chapters. A reproducible documentary assessment rubric is provided to assist you in both focusing student effort and assessing the quality of their work at each of the four phases of the process.

Directors create documentary films to share with others. In chapter 7, a number of options for sharing and celebrating student work are overviewed. Whether you host a classroom or school-wide film festival, share student work online, or encourage students to enter one of several film competitions, it is a wonderful culminating activity for students to share their work with a wider audience. Issues of privacy and copyright should be considered in determining the scope and medium for sharing student work.

The book concludes with advice from other teachers. Chapter 8 includes tips, guidance, and lessons learned from teachers at several grade levels in a number of schools. In this chapter, you'll find both very pragmatic advice related to making the process work and more-philosophical issues you may want to consider in creating your own classroom documentary project.

CREDITS

Normally, credits come at the end of a film, but we knew the establishing shot of this book needed to feature our many colleagues who made this project possible. From documentarians to teachers to social studies educators, we have many people to thank for their contributions, insights, and collaborations over the past ten years. They have challenged and expanded our thinking, trusted us with their students, and provided endless rounds of feedback, suggestions, and ideas. This book would not have been possible without the support of:

- Katie Booth, Scott County High School, Georgetown, Kentucky
- Julie Bray, Toano Middle School, Williamsburg, Virginia
- David Carpenter, Washington International School, Washington, DC
- Lauren Colley, University of Kentucky, Lexington, Kentucky
- Bruce Fehn, University of Iowa, Iowa City, Iowa
- Lauren Gallicchio, Bryan Station High School, Lexington, Kentucky
- Jen Garrott, Colonial Williamsburg Foundation, Williamsburg, Virginia
- S. G. Grant, Binghamton University, Binghamton, New York
- Tom Hammond, Lehigh University, Pennsylvania
- Joseph Karb, Springville-Griffith Middle School
- Jason Howard, Woodford High School, Versailles, Kentucky
- John Lee, North Carolina State University, North Carolina
- Benjamin Higgins, Springville-Griffith Middle School
- Linda Levstik, University of Kentucky, Lexington, Kentucky

- Meghan Manfra, North Carolina State University, North Carolina
- Julie Marsh, College of William and Mary, Williamsburg, Virginia
- Joan Mazur, University of Kentucky, Lexington, Kentucky
- Sean Moran, Director of Technology for Washington International School
- Rebecca Mueller, University of Kentucky, Lexington, Kentucky
- Robb Ponton, Rawls Byrd Elementary School, Williamsburg, Virginia
- Richard Satchwell, Midwest Center for Teaching with Primary Sources, Library of Congress
- Candace Schafer-Southard, Warhill High School, Williamsburg, Virginia
- Jim Schul, Ohio Northern University, Ada, Ohio
- Kim Tabler, Maryville Elementary, Bullitt County, Kentucky
- Kelly Tellech, Rosa Parks Elementary School, Lexington, Kentucky
- Emma Thacker, University of Kentucky, Lexington, Kentucky
- Abby Thurman, Shelby County Elementary School, Shelbyville, Kentucky
- James Walsh, Scott County High School, Georgetown, Kentucky
- Sharon Zuber, College of William & Mary, Williamsburg, Virginia

This book was made possible by not only the collaborators above but also by our families, who provided the support and motivation to spend our time tinkering with documentary making. Both parents of school-age children, we want Gray, Ben, and Emilia to come home beaming with excitement about the meaningful experiences they are having in their own social studies classroom. And of course, there are our respective spouses, Gerry and Eliana, who allow us to bat around ideas at night, when they would, we are certain, like us to be focusing on what's for dinner and who is taking whom to soccer practice. We thank them for allowing us to merge home and work life at times and for giving us the space to explore writing our first book.

1

SETTING THE SCENE

A Rationale for Student
Documentaries in the Classroom

When people talk to me about the digital divide, I think of it not being so much about who has access to what technology as who knows how to create and express themselves in this new language of the screen. If students aren't taught the language of sound and images, shouldn't they be considered as illiterate as if they left college without being able to read or write?

—George Lucas[1]

According the Kaiser Family Foundation, kids' media consumption is through the roof. Kids between the ages of 8 and 14 view nearly four and a half hours of television a day, and they spend an additional hour and a half per day on computers and video games.[2] This media immersion is seen as a defining characteristic of the millennial generation.

Prensky considers these students to be "digital natives," explaining that "our students today are all 'native speakers' of the digital language of computers, video games and the Internet."[3] Prensky's assumption is that it is incumbent upon teachers to leverage media, social networking tools, games, and other technology tools and resources to effectively teach this generation of digital natives. This presents opportunities and challenges for teachers as they grapple to integrate an expanding tool kit of technology applications and resources and to do so in a way that enhances students' abilities to "create and express themselves in this new language of the screen."[4]

The technology possibilities are endless for teachers, as is the expectation to integrate technology into the social studies classroom, particularly with the growing emphasis on 21st-century skills in schools. On the one hand, it seems that every day a new Web resource, mobile app, or software title is introduced, expanding the possibilities of what can be done in the classroom.

For example, a Web community like *ePals* enables teachers to form partnerships with other teachers from around the world to collaborate on classroom projects to engage in data collection, research, and debates. One very popular Web resource for U.S. history and government teachers is *The Living Room Candidate*, a portal that enables users to access, search, and filter thousands of presidential campaign commercials from every U.S. presidential election beginning in 1952. Other online databases like the *CIA World Factbook* and *Gapminder* allow students to compare and contrast geographic, political, economic, and social data from hundreds of countries. Clearly, these emerging and established technologies exponentially expand the number of resources and instructional opportunities for social studies teachers today.

On the other hand, this onrush of technology tools and resources can be overwhelming. First, many teachers feel inundated with the sheer number of choices, making it difficult to know where to start and how to fit these tools into the reality of day-to-day teaching. Second, even for those who keep pace with the newest gadgets or apps, it's easy to get fixated on the tools themselves. For example, it's tempting when finding a really interesting Web site to immediately figure out where it will fit into tomorrow's lesson rather than spending time exploring how, if at all, it strengthens the teaching and learning of social studies.

This kind of "technocentric" thinking may lead to a well-connected learning opportunity for our students, but it can also lead to using a tool for the sake of using the tool. In a standards-based teaching reality, teachers cannot afford the time to be trendy. More importantly, good teaching is rooted in purposeful and thoughtful construction of student experiences rather than in particular tools or resources.

Teachers who are able to use technology in ways that connect deeply with the social studies disciplines help to make this point. A high school teacher recently shared his efforts at integrating Twitter into his advanced placement government course. He created a private Twitter feed for his students that helped them stay current on the 2012 U.S. presidential election. He re-tweeted news from the candidates and the students tweeted to each other about issues the candidates raised during the televised debates.

The teacher explained that Twitter is both a new medium for political discourse and that the network helps him connect the conversations nationally to those globally—think Arab spring and the "central role" that social media played in revolutionary movements that toppled governments in Tunisia and Egypt in 2011.[5] He asserts that the Twitter feed helped make conversations about political discourse authentic and meaningful to the students and motivated his students to stay informed.

Unfortunately, when many teachers attempt to leverage social media or other technologies from pop culture (e.g., Facebook, Pinterest, Wordle, etc.), they do not always connect as well to disciplinary teaching and learning. In some cases, technologies can be what we like to call "green pancakes." This is a way to characterize learning activities that connect only superficially with the curricular objectives for a lesson.

For example, while studying the historical and cultural traditions of Ireland, a teacher might have the students make green pancakes. These pancakes might taste good and capture the students' attention, but the inclusion of the pancakes adds little value in helping the students to understand Irish culture.

While the use of some technologies in the classroom can be engaging and entertaining, to make the best use of these tools and resources, teachers must go beyond engagement and motivation to ensure that they add value to the learning experience.

STRATEGIC USE OF TECHNOLOGY IN CLASSROOMS

Given this challenge of staying abreast of the continual evolution of technology tools and resources and the inherent challenges of connecting them in substantive ways to curriculum-based teaching and learning, it makes sense to ask the question why consider using technology in our teaching, and documentary making in particular.

Unlike some professors, consultants, and vendors who work in educational technology, it is important that teachers begin with a healthy dose of skepticism toward classroom-based uses of technology. The extra time, effort, ambiguity, and complications that can often arise in using new tools and resources in the highly complex world of the K–12 classroom should make teachers very deliberate and discerning in their choices to integrate technology in their teaching. There should be a compelling reason to consider the adoption of technology in instructional practice.

Among others, there are three reasons social studies teachers might make the leap to integrate technology in their teaching: technology tools can help students develop 21st-century skills; technology can be used to address the common state standards in English language arts and social studies; and, most importantly, technology can provide both motivation and opportunities to engage students in disciplinary practices in the social studies disciplines.

21st-Century Skills

The students in K–12 classrooms today are entering a very different world than the ones in which many of their teachers grew up. The increasingly connected global economy puts a premium on workers who can collaborate, problem solve, network with colleagues at a distance, and continually learn new skills. Many of these skills and processes either require or are augmented through the use of digital technologies.

The logic goes that the more prepared our students are to use technology to engage in these 21st-century skills, the more competitive they will be in the global marketplace. The Partnership for 21st Century Skills (P21) offers a framework that suggests helping students develop the following skills in the context of their content-based learning experiences:

- Creativity and innovation
- Critical thinking and problem solving
- Communication and collaboration
- Information literacy
- Media literacy
- Information and communications technology (ICT) literacy

Teachers have integrated many of these skills for decades both with and without technology, but new technologies expand how these skills can be addressed in K–12 classrooms. What is important in the P21 framework, however, is that these skills should not be taught in isolation, but as a means to assist students in their curriculum-based learning.

Teachers routinely utilize a number of technologies to connect 21st-century skills with curriculum content. For example, students may work in teams to research a topic gathering Web-based resources, use a collaborative word processing tool to share their notes and information, and develop a wiki site together to share their understanding.

In other instances, a classroom of students in the United States might connect with Web conferencing tools (e.g., Skype, Facetime) with students from China to discuss similarities and differences in the political systems, cultural traditions, and daily life in their respective countries. Finally, students may conduct field research by recording interviews with local business owners to ascertain the current state of the local economy and produce an NPR-style podcast. In all these examples, students are using appropriate technology tools to develop the kinds of skills that will help them be successful in the world while concurrently addressing valuable social studies skills and concepts.

Some proponents of these 21st-century skills argue that they are so important for students that they should be considered ends in themselves. However, both the current focus on standardized curriculum and high-stakes testing and the inherent value in disciplinary concepts and skills make it incumbent upon teachers to find ways to *integrate* these skills in curriculum-based teaching and learning. As the examples noted above illustrate, these skills can certainly be engendered within the context of meaningful, content-based classroom experiences.

Common Standards in English Language Arts and Social Studies

With the widespread adoption of the Common Core English Language Arts standards across the country, social studies teachers in 46 states are now required to teach literacy skills within the social studies classroom.[6] Many educators are already doing this but with these new standards in place, all teachers are being asked to explicitly draw connections between the skills laid out within the Common Core State Standards for English Language Arts and the social studies curriculum.

These standards specify reading, speaking and listening, language, and writing skills that must be demonstrated at each grade level but ultimately delineate those literacy skills and understandings that students need to demonstrate by high school graduation. The architects of the Common Core State Standards emphasize the close reading of informational text and emphasize the critical role that social studies plays in building the skills necessary to "evaluate intricate arguments, synthesize complex information, and follow detailed descriptions of events and concepts."[7]

Technology is uniquely situated to help teachers do some of these things that are expressed in Common Core English Language Arts (ELA) Standards. For example, in the College and Career Readiness Anchor Standards for Reading, the standards include:

- Reading closely to determine what the text says explicitly and to make logical inferences from it and then citing specific textual evidence when writing or speaking to support conclusions drawn from the text.[8]
- Assessing how point of view or purpose shapes the content and style of a text.[9]
- Integrating and evaluating content presented in diverse formats and media, including visually and quantitatively, as well as in words.[10]
- Analyzing how two or more texts address similar themes or topics in order to build knowledge or to compare the approaches the authors take.[11]

Web-based archives of primary and secondary source documents (including text, still images, audio, and video) provide teachers and students with a wealth of possibilities for a wide range of reading materials. Using annotation features in word processing software (i.e., comments in Word or Google Docs) as well as Web page annotation tools (e.g., *Diigo* and *Scrible*) allows students opportunities to highlight passages, make connections between passages, and share their notes.

Technologies can also assist students as they practice the following skills within the College and Career Readiness Anchor Standards for Writing:

- Writing arguments to support claims in an analysis of substantive topics or texts using valid reasoning and relevant and sufficient evidence.[12]
- Writing narratives to develop real or imagined experiences or events using effective technique, well-chosen details, and well-structured event sequences.[13]
- Using technology, including the Internet, to produce and publish writing and to interact and collaborate with others.[14]
- Conducting short, as well as more sustained, research projects based on focused questions, demonstrating understanding of the subject under investigation.[15]
- Gathering relevant information from multiple print and digital sources, assessing the credibility and accuracy of each source, and integrating the information while avoiding plagiarism.[16]

The multitude of authoring tools available through publishing applications (e.g., word processing and audio and video creation software) and Web-based creation, sharing, and curation tools (e.g., Glogster, VoiceThread, wikis, blogs, and podcasts) enable students to create their own writing products in a variety of modes, supporting the differentiation of both process and product. Additionally, many of these tools also allow for collaboration and publishing for others to access the work. These and other technologies not only support the integration of Common Core State Standards in the social studies disciplines; in many cases, they extend and amplify the goals embedded in the standards.

The recently published College, Career, and Civic Life (C3) Framework for Social Studies State Standards also emphasizes the use of multimodal technologies as a means for producing the results or conclusions of an inquiry.[17] In Dimension 2 of the C3 Framework, students are expected to use a variety of discipline-specific tools to investigate the four core social studies disciplines of civics, economics, geography, and history. For example, students studying geography are expected to use geospatial and other technology tools to explain spatial patterns and cultural and environmental characteristics of a place or region. Aligning with the literacy standards, in Dimension 3, students gather sources using Web-based search engines and databases, and in Dimension 4, students are encouraged to produce conclusions to their inquiries using multimodal technologies. To be college and career ready, students need to meet these technology-performance expectations woven throughout the C3 Framework and the Common Core State Standards for ELA.

Connections with the Disciplines

One way to keep the focus on classroom learning when considering educational technologies is through focusing on those tools and resources that are particularly well connected to the disciplinary concepts and skills embedded in the social studies disciplines. These technologies are authentic to the disciplines. For this reason, they can be considered *specialized* tools.[18] This does not, however, preclude the use of *universal* tools that can also support social studies instruction.

Universal tools are more general in nature and do not explicitly connect with a particular discipline (e.g., history, geography, or economics). For example, multimedia presentation and word processing software, document cameras, interactive whiteboards, and Web-based streaming video can be used in a variety of content areas and disciplines. In our own research, we have examined the use of podcasting and PowerPoint to support students' communication of content knowledge in economics and history. These tools can provide students with varied means to access content and help them share their understandings, but do not assist students in thinking more historically, for instance.

Specialized technologies provide opportunities for teachers and their students to engage with the disciplines in powerful, authentic ways. In the following examples, the use of a specialized tool is detailed in each of the four core social studies disciplines:

- In civics, students can explore the legislative and voting processes in the Youth Leadership Initiative *eCongress* and *Mock Elections*.
- In economics, students can use sites like *Gapminder* and software like *Excel* or *InspireData* to explore and visualize relationships between data.
- In geography, students can explore spatial patterns by accessing geographic information systems (GIS) or GIS-enabled Web sites to both explore and create dynamic, annotated, data-based maps.

- In history, students can access the same digital archives of historical documents that historians use to research and explore questions; students can also find primary and secondary sources to support their own research and analysis.

These are just some of the specialized tools and resources that offer opportunities to engage students in discipline-based thinking. What these all have in common is the clear connection between the tool and the content. In many cases, these sites and resources have been created for K–12 students in collaboration with social scientists. As a result, they reflect important disciplinary concepts and thinking structures.

When teachers connect student work with these kinds of disciplinary ways of thinking, they are engaging their students in what Fred M. Newmann and his colleagues from the University of Wisconsin call *authentic intellectual work* (AIW). The AIW framework outlines teaching and learning that "involves original application of knowledge and skills, rather than just routine use of facts and procedures. It also entails careful study of the details of a particular topic or problem and results in a product or presentation that has meaning beyond success in school."[19] The AIW framework for assessing student work is divided into three dimensions: construction of knowledge, conceptual understanding, and elaborated communication.

To demonstrate construction of knowledge in the AIW framework, student work should exhibit "interpretation, analysis, synthesis, or evaluation to construct knowledge, rather than merely retrieving or restating Social Studies facts, concepts, and definitions given by the teacher or other sources."[20] This can be achieved when students connect ideas and themes between periods in history, develop arguments related to social issues, or analyze data in a variety of forms.

Conceptual understanding challenges students to go beyond facts, figures, and data to develop understanding related to the big ideas in the discipline. When students demonstrate "understanding of important Social Studies concepts by *using them to explain historical and contemporary events* [emphasis added], social data and trends, public policies, or to take positions on social issues,"[21] they are engaged in building their conceptual understanding.

Often students are asked to communicate what they understand about a particular topic or unit through a quiz or test or an essay, or through the development of a project. In many cases, however, they don't have opportunities to bring in multiple forms of evidence, media, or genres in conveying this understanding. Providing students opportunities for elaborated communication allows students to draw on examples, illustrations, details, and evidence (e.g., video recorded speeches, census data) to convey a more nuanced understanding of a course topic or idea.

Engaging students in this kind of thinking can be motivating both on the intellectual and affective levels. While this kind of work may be more challenging than what they are typically asked to do, through the use of provocative questions or experiences, students find this work very meaningful. Documentary filmmaking is one powerful way to engage students in authentic intellectual work in the social studies.

THE UNIQUE POTENTIAL OF DOCUMENTARY MAKING

Classroom documentary making is particularly interesting because strategic efforts in this area can address all three technology-enhanced opportunities that are discussed above (i.e., 21st-century skills, common state standards, and disciplinary connections). In the process of creating documentaries, students work collaboratively to research their topics using a variety of sources and develop a nuanced, multimodal narrative of the topic that they communicate through the creation of digital video that can be shared online. Moreover, these skills are developed in the context of the kinds of disciplinary thinking essential to the social studies classroom.

Documentary creation is a compelling technology in the social studies, as it has elements of both a specialized and universal tool. While moviemaking technology is used across the curricula, from English language arts to mathematics, documentary films are a common and evocative medium through which social scientists present their interpretations of social phenomena.

A quick review of the documentary category in the Netflix directory offers dozens of examples including *The War*; *Inside Job*; *Food, Inc.*; *Waiting for Superman*; and *Maxed Out*. In these varied films, social scientists are at work creating evidence-based interpretations grounded in the norms and rules of disciplinary work. So, in this way, while the digital tools used to create documentary films are universal, the process by which directors create their films can be deeply rooted in disciplinary concepts and skills.

Despite this unique potential of documentaries, there are many examples of good ideas for the classroom (technology or otherwise) that seem quite promising, but don't always translate well to classroom practice (who remembers the call for education to move to Second Life?). So, while documentary making rationally seems like a good fit for the social studies classroom, it is essential to take an honest look at how it plays out in authentic classroom settings.

Our research on classroom-based digital documentary creation over the past 10 years has occured in standards-based, high stakes–testing classrooms.[22] We learned a great deal from our teacher collaborators with each successive documentary effort. You will meet a number of these teachers throughout the book through examples, sidebars, and case studies. Many of the projects have been quite successful, but these efforts have not always been easy or without difficulties. In fact, for several years, it seemed like there emerged a new challenge with each successive project.

In order to refine the process and iron out some of the challenges documented in the research literature, the documentary production process outlined in this book is a result of partnerships with filmmakers, historians, educational technologists, and classroom teachers with experience in leading documentary projects. This book is a direct result of these collaborations. This process and book have been created to assist social studies educators to efficiently and effectively structure and assess documentary projects in ways that help students engage in disciplined inquiry in a way that leverages the unique potential of filmmaking.

THE CHALLENGE AHEAD

In elementary, middle school, and high school classrooms, it is clear how powerful student-created documentaries can be. Students are motivated to work on their films before and after school and during their lunch periods, and choose to take much of their work home. This book will offer you a number of student-created examples that demonstrate the creativity, nuance, and depth with which students can communicate their understanding in this medium.

Unfortunately, these projects can also flounder, making some teachers wonder if the project was worth the effort. The reality is, this is difficult work. Within a documentary project, students will steer off course and wander in and out of their research question; teachers will struggle to manage multiple student projects while guiding an iterative research, writing, and production process; and inevitably, technology will fail—either shutting down at just the wrong moment, blocking a particularly interesting Web site, or simply not doing what you want it to *when* you want it to.

As such, leading a documentary project requires an extra dose of patience, measured enthusiasm, increased organization, and the willingness to work through the inevitable challenges of producing a student-created product. In the case of documentary making, technology might make some parts of the task better, but not necessarily easier.

CONCLUSION

Our challenge to you is this: Be ambitious, but also be realistic. Don't be afraid to start small and grow a documentary project from the fundamentals of good social studies teaching—disciplinary inquiry, research, and argumentation. As you read through the following chapters, think about the critical elements of the process that are essential for *your* students. If this is your first time creating documentaries, stick to the basics. If you have been at this awhile, perhaps you will find some additional strategies to layer onto your own process or to fix something that hasn't gone quite right in your classroom.

Throughout the rest of the book, you will learn about a four-stage process for documentary making from teachers who have done well with documentaries, but also from those who have struggled at various stages. Throughout this book, you will be introduced to a number of classroom examples that will help you determine whether the extra time and energy is worth it in the case of documentary making for your students. And even though you might feel a bit overwhelmed, this book will provide you with both a road map and a tool kit of instructional resources to give you the confidence and courage to lead a project in your own classroom.

NOTES

1. James Daley, "Life on the Screen: Visual Literacy in Education," *Edutopia* (2004): accessed May 8, 2013. http://www.edutopia.org/lucas-visual-literacy.

2. Kaiser Family Foundation, "Generation M2: Media in the Lives of 8- to 18-Year-Olds," *Author*, January 20, 2010, http://kff.org/other/event/generation-m2-media-in-the-lives-of/

3. Marc Prensky, "Digital Natives, Digital Immigrants," *On the Horizon* 9, no. 5 (2001): 1–6.

4. James Daley, "Life on the Screen: Visual Literacy in Education," *Edutopia* (2004). Accessed May 8, 2013, http://www.edutopia.org/lucas-visual-literacy

5. Philip N. Howard, Aiden Duffy, Deen Freelon, Muzammil Hussain, Will Mari, and Marwa Mazaid, "Opening Closed Regimes: What Was the Role of Social Media During the Arab Spring?" *Project on Information Technology and Political Islam* (2012): 1–30. http://pitpi.org/wp-content/uploads/2013/02/2011_Howard-Duffy-Freelon-Hussain-Mari-Mazaid_pITPI.pdf

6. National Governors Association Center for Best Practices and Council of Chief State School Officers, *Common Core State Standards for English Language Arts and Literacy in History/Social Studies, Science, and Technical Subjects* (Washington, DC: Author, 2010).

7. Ibid., 59.

8. Ibid., 60.

9. Ibid.

10. Ibid.

11. Ibid.

12. Ibid., 63.

13. Ibid.

14. Ibid.

15. Ibid.

16. Ibid.

17. National Council for the Social Studies, *The College, Career, and Civic Life (C3) Framework for Social Studies State Standards: Guidance for Enhancing the Rigor of K-12 Civics, Economics, Geography, and History* (NCSS, Washington, DC).

18. Kathy Swan and Mark Hofer, "In Search of Technological Pedagogical Content Knowledge (TPACK): Teachers' Initial Foray into Podcasting in Economics," *Journal of Research and Technology in Social Education* 44, no. 1 (2011): 53–73.

18. M. Bruce King, Fred M. Newmann, and Dana L. Carmichael, "Authentic Intellectual Work: Common Standards for Teaching Social Studies," *Social Education* 68, no. 3 (2009): 44.

20. Ibid., 58.

21. Ibid., 60.

22. Andrew Burn, Sue Brindley, James Durran, Carol Kelsall, Jane Sweetlove, and Caroline Tuohey, "The Rush of Images: A Research Report into Digital Editing and the Moving Image," *English in Education* 35, no. 2 (2001): 34–48. doi:10.1111/j.1754-8845.2001.tb00739.x; Helen Hoffenberg and Marianne Handler, "Digital Video Goes to School," *Learning and Leading with Technology* 29, no. 2 (2001): 10–15; Mark Hofer and Kathy Swan, "Technological Pedagogical Content Knowledge from the Ground Level: A Case Study of a Middle School Digital Documentary Project," *Journal of Research and Technology Education* 41, no. 2 (2008): 179–200; Kathy Swan and Mark Hofer, "Digital Campaigning: Using the Bill of Rights to Advance a Political Position," *The Social Studies* 97, no. 5 (2006): 208–214. doi:10.3200/TSSS.97.5; Kathy Swan, Mark Hofer, and Linda S. Levstik, "And Action! Students Collaborating in the Digital Directors Guild," *Social Studies and the Young Learner* 19, no. 4 (2007): 17–20; Matthew Kearney and Sandy Schuck, "Authentic Learning Through the Use of Digital Video" (presentation, Australasian Computing Education Conference, Adelaide, Australia, July 2004). http://hdl.handle.net/10453/7451; Jennifer New, "Film School: Making Movies from Storyboard to Screen," *Edutopia* 19, no. 1 (2006): 20–23; Mark Reid, Andrew Burn, and David Parker, *Evaluation Report of the BECTA Digital Video Pilot Project* (Coventry, UK: British Educational Communications and Technology Agency, 2002); Stepben Ryan, "Digital Video: Using Technology to Improve Learner Motivation," *Modern English Teacher* 11, no. 2 (2002): 72–75; Kathy Swan, Mark Hofer, and Gerry Swan, "Examining Authentic Intellectual Work with a Social Studies Digital Documentary Inquiry Project in a Mandated State-Testing Environment," *Journal of Digital Learning in Teacher Education* 27, no. 3 (2011): 115–122; Kathy Swan and Mark Hofer, "Examining Student-Created Documentaries as a Mechanism for Engaging Students in Authentic Intellectual Work," *Theory and Research in Social Education* 40, no. 1 (2013): 133–175; Sonja Yow & Kathy Swan, "If You Build It, Should I Run? A Teacher's Perspective on Implementing a Student-Centered Technology Project in His Ninth-Grade Geography Classroom," in *Research on Technology and Social Studies Education*, eds. John Lee and Adam M. Friedman (Charlotte, NC: Information Age Publishing, 2009), 155–172.

2

WRITING WITH LIGHT

Preparing for a Documentary Project

One of the great things about being a director as a life choice is that it can never be mastered. Every story is its own kind of expedition, with its own set of challenges.

—Ron Howard[1]

Classroom documentary projects can engage students in constructing evidence-based arguments as well as in developing essential literacies and 21st-century skills in ways that clearly connect with the core purposes and practices of social studies. However, student documentary making is an intricate and layered learning process that requires pre-teaching of skills (e.g., gathering sources, evaluating evidence, developing claims and counterclaims) as well as a variety of scaffolds in the form of teacher feedback (both formative and summative) throughout the filmmaking project.[2]

Although documentary making is worth doing, successful projects are dependent upon thoughtful planning and implementation that includes an honest discussion of how projects can go wrong and how to avoid common pedagogical pitfalls.

In this chapter, we outline a four-phase production process that was developed to guide students in creating documentaries. These four phases mirror how professional filmmakers approach their craft in a way that helps teachers to structure the process to help guide their students to create substantive documentaries.

In the remainder of the chapter, this four-phase process is described with a corresponding assessment rubric that was developed collaboratively with teachers, technology specialists, teacher educators, and filmmakers. The chapter ends with a discussion of the importance of considering your unique classroom context in the planning process.

SHIFTING PEDAGOGY

Several early efforts in classroom documentary creation resulted in student films that resembled electronic encyclopedia entries.[3] While still worthwhile, many of these projects did not capitalize on the opportunities afforded by documentary making. After examining the student products and the processes that led to the creation of these films, it became clear that teachers were struggling to shift pedagogy from guiding students in writing an expository essay to making a documentary. Not surprisingly, students essentially wrote an essay, which they set to music and shoehorned images into the narrative as an afterthought. In doing so, they failed to take advantage of the visual and aural power of documentaries.

Even though the students were actively engaged in the work, one wonders whether all the extra time and effort on the part of the teachers was really worth it given that students could have just as easily written a paper or developed a PowerPoint presentation. What separates a film from these other kinds of products is the *potential* for both the aesthetic possibilities and the story-driven nature of documentary films.

It's no wonder that teachers have difficulty in making this pedagogical shift given that filmmaking is its own discipline whose unique processes are typically unfamiliar to teachers and students. Although students consume a great deal of media today, they are not necessarily savvy creators of educational media. This is also true in schools.

As teachers work to integrate new technologies into teaching, it is natural that they would appropriate these tools using instructional strategies, like expository writing, that are more familiar. It became evident that more information about how filmmakers approach their work was needed to develop an understanding of the process and skills required of teachers and students in this new medium. This collaboration focused on two key elements: being deliberate and thoughtful about the visual elements of the film and on merging evidence-based argument with storytelling techniques.

A NEW MEDIUM—VISUAL VS. VERBAL

Initial meetings with the documentarians revealed a key issue that needed to be accounted for in the documentary process. Unlike written documents, the primary mode of communication in film is visual. In early classroom documentary projects, the primary emphasis was placed on the research and written script. The documentarians, however, argued that first and foremost, students needed to move directly from the research phase to selecting images that help to tell their story. They then can iteratively progress bringing together a script with the emergent visual text.

After viewing a classroom set of these early documentaries, one of the filmmakers, Sharon Zuber, explained the primacy of images and the shift that needed to take place as students learned how to "write with light":[4]

> There were two key challenges: Trying to downplay the written narration so that students were thinking visually, not just verbally, then helping students match up the narrative with the visual images themselves. In education, we are very reliant on the written word even though we live in such a visual culture; helping both students and teachers shift to paying attention first to images is really important to move them away from our verbal culture to using visual language.[5]

Filmmakers use argument and narrative as part of the writing process but include an additional skill set when making films. "Writing with light" is a literal translation of the word "photography," which suggests a rich history and tradition of comparisons between print and visual mediums. This translation hints at the interconnected nature of writing and filmmaking. Filmmaking is essentially a new form of writing that creates a visual experience for the viewer, but it is still a form of writing.

For a director, this means starting the documentary creation process by thinking visually as well as verbally. By first selecting images that are evocative and vivid, the documentarian is able to not just tell a story but also show the story as it unfolds before its audience. In fact, the famous documentarian

Ken Burns has his own effect in Apple's iMovie called the Ken Burns effect in which a filmmaker can apply Burns's technique of zooming and panning over a still image, slowly and deliberately, to create motion but also to focus the audience on the meaning of a compelling scene or person.

Not surprisingly, the selection and sequencing of images is often subordinate to the writing process in most classroom iterations. Teachers typically begin the documentary process with the familiar—as strictly a writing exercise followed by a Google image search to illustrate the text with images. In doing so, the student is often forced into making less than ideal choices for the film, as the narrative is disconnected to a particular image, and where the image does not contribute to the overall interpretation.

Within the documentary process that follows, students will work through an "image rough cut" to place a more deliberate emphasis on visuals to support the interpretation that students construct early on in the production. See chapter 5 for further explanation, strategies, templates, and techniques for introducing the image rough cut to students.

BUILDING AN INTERPRETATION: MERGING STORYTELLING AND EVIDENCE-BASED ARGUMENT

One other way that documentary films tend to be different from essays and other typical written work is that they tell a story. Some think of documentaries as factual accounts of a particular person or event, but this isn't necessarily true. Instead, a filmmaker tries to find the story to tell related to a particular person, event, or issue. Documentaries have a particular point of view and message they hope to convey. This interpretation is supported with examples, quotations, data, and other forms of support or evidence. In essence, documentaries become an amalgam of storytelling and evidence-based arguments in a visual format.

Teachers and students often have more experience with conventional persuasive writing than with the documentary experience. Students are taught in elementary school the five-paragraph essay format—sometimes known as the "hamburger model," where there is thesis (the top bun), main points (the hamburger), supporting details (the fixings including tomato, lettuce, pickles, and onions), and then finally a restatement of the thesis (bottom bun). Teachers employ a number of strategies to help their students write using various scaffolding techniques and templates to help them to clearly communicate their argument.

Filmmakers have a similar goal, but take a slightly different approach to structuring and conveying their arguments. Rather than using conventional writing techniques, they rely on the ancient Greek *rule of fourths* and *story arc* to help tell their stories in a way that is compelling to the audience. A careful examination of documentary films (short form or long form) reveals that they are typically structured in three acts: the introduction, the body, and the conclusion.

The rule of fourths suggests that the introduction and conclusion each comprise roughly one-fourth of the total runtime of the film and the body comprises the middle two-fourths of the film. The introduction essentially sets the stage for the film, often introducing the context and struggle, or challenge, central to the story. There is usually some type of turning, or transition, point following the introduction that sets the protagonist on a journey.

The middle section of the film then follows an arc in which the action rises, leading to the second turning, or transition, point. It is in this body section that the filmmaker uses evidence and examples to support the story or argument. Following the second turning, or transition, point, the conclusion offers some type of resolution to the story.

This storytelling aspect is one of the key ways in which films are different from the typical work students do in social studies classrooms. The story is what makes documentaries both engaging and persuasive.

Clearly there was a need to bridge the thinking and processes of filmmakers with the K–12 classroom experience. In a series of interviews with the documentarians, four distinct but fluid stages of the documentary process began to emerge. These steps are instructionally sequential and allow for formative checkpoints along the documentary production timeline.

In the next section of the chapter, there is an overview of the documentary production process. Within the descriptions of each stage, there is a short definition and a brief outline of the important activities that students would engage in during the four phases. Please note, though, that each of these phases will be explained in further detail in later chapters, including multiple classroom examples of how teachers have used this process in their own practice.

A DOCUMENTARY PROCESS

Phase 1: Research

Filmmakers begin a documentary by exploring a question, gathering and evaluating information, and crafting a response or argument to the question. In Phase 1, students begin similarly with guiding or supporting questions that challenge them to move beyond information gathering to incorporate analysis that builds toward a point of view. At the end of this phase, students develop an outline of their argument that includes supporting points and evidence.

Phase 2: Documentary Treatment

Practicing documentarians begin the pre-production process by developing a documentary treatment. Students in this phase complete a documentary treatment template in which they develop a "pitch" for their film that includes an interesting theme, appropriate narrative structure, and a probing question that the student filmmakers would like the audience to explore. Included within the treatment is an outline of the film that lays out the sequencing of ideas and the architecture of the film.

Phase 3: Storyboard

In the storyboard process, filmmakers embellish the documentary treatment to include all the elements in the movie frame (e.g., visuals, sound, narration, effects)—essentially a blueprint for the production of the film. Students in this phase create an image rough cut, develop a script for narration and onscreen text, and identify the music and visual effects for use in the film. At the end of this phase, students complete a digital or paper copy of a storyboard for their film including all of the elements referenced above.

Phase 4: Film Production

In the production process, filmmakers assemble their films and bring the vision of the storyboard to the screen. At the end of this phase, students export their video project (using whatever tools are available) as a video file.

In subsequent chapters, each of the four phases is discussed in more detail, and there are templates and classroom examples of how the phases have worked in a variety of classroom settings.

It is important to note that the audience for this book is classroom social studies teachers, not professional filmmakers. This book is designed to appropriate filmmaking elements from professional documentarians and translate these to a typical classroom setting. This approach is not an attempt to create professional documentaries—rather, by borrowing important tools, concepts, and practices from the filmmaking genre, the documentary process in classrooms improves and ultimately becomes more authentic.

This is an important distinction, as these stages may be unfamiliar or somewhat limited to filmmakers. However, teachers should find this translation helpful in guiding students through an unfamiliar process that is constrained by money (students certainly do not have a Ken Burns budget), time (at some point, the bell rings and students must go to their next class), skill (students are learning these skills and thus need scaffolds in the early stages), and technology (state-of-the-art equipment in schools is a rarity).

DESIGNING A RUBRIC

A number of classroom teachers and filmmakers have collaborated to develop the process as well as an accompanying assessment (See Appendix A). Because students are engaged in a variety of writing, research, and analytic processes before they produce their final films, teachers need a way to assess the formative work, as well as the summative product, in order to monitor the work as students move through the documentary-making process. Without this multistaged assessment, teachers are forced into making a number of inferences about the students' understanding and analytical processes.[6]

The assessment at the end of each phase can serve as an opportunity for the teacher to provide key instruction so that if the work was unacceptable, inaccurate, or going down the wrong path, they could direct the student back into the narrative so that the research, analysis, and interpretation are central to the documentary process. This formative assessment is important to ensure that students are completing each phase with fidelity so that Phase 4, film production, serves as a carrot, or incentive, in the assessment process. In other words, students postpone the motivating production process (e.g., selecting transitions, creating or identifying effective music and sound elements, etc.) until they have done the hard work of researching and writing.

As a result of these conversations, the rubric was developed to correspond with the four phases of the documentary process. A study of the construct and face validities of the rubric suggests that this rubric is effective and valid in measuring key aspects of documentary creation.[7] Teachers will certainly modify or emphasize/deemphasize certain elements (e.g., collecting student note cards in the research phase rather than using guiding questions; a bulleted overview of the film rather than a traditional documentary treatment), but this multiphased assessment of student work will enable teachers to more accurately assess student learning.

In the following four chapters, the components of the rubric are unpacked in greater detail with a comprehensive collection of instructional materials, including a production process and time line, a documentary treatment and storyboard template, brief help guides (e.g., developing a story arc, film production and editing techniques, etc.), and student examples that will support you in planning for and implementing a classroom documentary project as well as assist you in assessing the stages and dimensions of students' work.

FACTORING IN CONTEXT

While this phased approach discussed above will help you to effectively structure your documentary project, each classroom is unique. The context in which you will lead the project should be carefully considered so that you can implement and modify the suggestions for each phase in the chapters that follow. In this section, elements of your classroom context are highlighted so that you can begin to plan your project. Please note, however, that the ideas are merely introduced here. You will have the opportunity to consider these parameters in more depth and will have the benefit of seeing how other teachers have approached the challenge in the chapters that follow.

CURRICULUM FOCUS

As noted in chapter 1, in this era of accountability and high-stakes testing, it is critically important that the documentary project should address core curriculum concepts and skills. When selecting a curricular focus for the documentary project, you may want to strategically identify potential units that lend themselves to a documentary project. These may be units with relatively more class time allotted to cover the content, units that lend themselves to exploration of multiple points of view around a topic through the use of historical documents, or units for which you would like to utilize a project-based approach. As you think about a curricular focus, also consider particular skills (e.g., image or primary source analysis, argument development, or oral communication) that may lend themselves to the creation of a documentary film.

TIME

Time is a precious commodity in classrooms today. You'll want to be sure that as you select a curricular focus that you will have enough time in your scope and sequence to accommodate a multiweek documentary project. In the chapters that follow, teachers will share their stories of how they have navigated this challenge, and there will be suggestions for how to streamline the process in a variety of ways. Still, you'll need to have the equivalent of a minimum of eight class periods to implement a documentary project in the classroom. More realistically, though, as many as 10 to 15 class periods may be required.

STUDENT LEARNING NEEDS AND PREFERENCES

Each class is different. Sometimes a particular group of students works very well in small groups; sometimes groups larger than pairs can lead to inefficiency and/or chaos. Some students may need structure in the form of specific roles within the group, multiple checkpoints with formative feedback, and a more template-driven approach, while others may thrive on a more emergent approach to the work. You may find that whole class feedback on drafts of the work is beneficial in some classes, while in others, feedback from the teacher along the way may be more productive.

As you think through the phases of the project, try to think about them with a specific class or classes of students in mind as you make instructional decisions. You may even find that you need to customize some phases of the project for a particular group of students that is somewhat different than other sections of the course. In the end, the more you can design the work with the particular strengths and challenges of your students in mind, the more successful you will be.

ACCESS TO TECHNOLOGY

While classroom access to technology has been rapidly increasing over the past 10 years, the reality is that schools (and sometimes different departments within schools) have varying degrees of access to technology. The tools, resources, and settings (i.e., laptops in the classroom or a computer lab) will have a considerable impact on how you design your project. For example, a documentary project in a one-computer classroom will look very different than one in a one-to-one laptop setting.

Don't think just in terms of access to computers, though. You might also want to do some research about additional technology tools and resources available to you during the project. Specifically, you may want to look for the following: headset microphones, network folders for students to save their work, access to online video services (e.g., Discovery Education or Safari Montage), digital audio recorders, and most especially, video editing software (e.g., Microsoft's Photo Story or Movie Maker, or Apple's iMovie).

A clear idea of the technology tools and resources available to you and your students will help to inform some of the instructional decisions you make—particularly in the research and production phases.

HUMAN RESOURCES

Perhaps more important even than access to tools and resources is an understanding of who in the school or district might be able to support you before and during the project. For example, the assistance of the school library media specialist can be extremely helpful in supporting you and your students in the research phase. Assistance from an English/language arts teacher can be very helpful both in structuring the script writing and in providing feedback on their process. A technology coordinator or integration specialist can be invaluable in terms of considering the technology alternatives, supporting students during the production phase, and assisting with the inevitable technical difficulties that you might encounter.

Don't forget the students themselves. Given the popularity of video-sharing sites like YouTube and Vimeo online, it is possible some of your students have already produced their own video projects. They can be wonderful "consultants" to the rest of the class during the project. Finally, you might also reach out to parents and other community members to draw on their expertise as well. It's important to remember that you can't possibly be an expert on every facet of a documentary project and that you're not alone.

A CAUTIONARY NOTE

A teacher's enthusiasm is a necessary ingredient to designing and implementing a classroom documentary project. However, enthusiasm alone is simply not enough to ensure a successful project. Careful planning and structure is essential to surviving and thriving in a documentary project. Keep the particulars of your classroom context in mind as you proceed through the following chapters on the phases of the process. Try to balance your ambition with reality of classroom practice. With careful planning and anticipation of possible challenges at each step of the process, you increase your chances of creating a successful learning experience for your students.

One teacher, Henry, admittedly overreached in his documentary project with students. After students finished the films he said:

> I tried to have a positive attitude but it dwindled rapidly as the project unfolded, largely because I bit off more than I could chew. I would even say that I was a hindrance to the project myself. I didn't do a good job of escorting the students through the baby steps. Inquiry was too tough to tackle in conjunction with the technology project.

This type of quote is difficult to share, but we want to underscore that documentary making, like any other elaborate learning experience, is not just a "drop-in activity" to the curriculum. Teachers should take into consideration all of the contextual factors that impact successful implementation.

LOOKING AHEAD

In the next chapter, you will explore Phase 1 of the documentary production process: research. A strong documentary project is grounded in guiding students through a research process. To understand the topic and find the story, substantive background knowledge is vitally important.

In this stage of the process, teachers help students move beyond a collection of note cards with isolated facts, concepts, and ideas. Instead, teachers must help students develop a rich, nuanced understanding of their topics that takes into account multiple perspectives and augment their background knowledge by gathering evidence (e.g., text, images, video, data tables, maps, charts) that can be used to support their arguments.

There is a discussion of how and why to cite sources in documentaries as well as suggestions for navigating copyright and fair use. The chapter concludes with the introduction of the first part of the assessment rubric that enables teachers to easily score the quality of student research and to provide formative assessment feedback.

NOTES

1. Charles S. Warn, "Ron Howard Weightless Again Over Apollo 13's DGA Win," DGA Magazine, accessed August 16, 2013, http://www.industrycentral.net/director_interviews/RH01.HTM.

2. Kathy Swan and Mark Hofer, "Examining Student-Created Documentaries as a Mechanism for Engaging Students in Authentic Intellectual Work," *Theory and Research in Social Education* 40, no. 1 (2013): 133–175.

3. Mark Hofer and Kathleen Owings-Swan, "Digital Moviemaking—The Harmonization of Technology, Pedagogy and Content," *International Journal of Technology in Teaching and Learning* 1, no. 1 (2005): 102–110.

4. Sharon Zuber, "Writing with Light," *Jump! Magazine* 17, no. 2 (1997): n.p.

5. Sharon Zuber, interview by Mark Hofer, 2011, interview transcript.

6. Kathy Swan and Mark Hofer, "In Search of Technological Pedagogical Content Knowledge (TPACK): Teachers' Initial Foray into Podcasting in Economics," *Journal of Research and Technology Education* 44, no. 1 (2011): 53–73.

7. Judith Arter and Jay McTighe, *Scoring Rubrics in the Classroom: Using Performance Criteria for Assessing and Improving Student Performance* (Thousand Oaks, CA: Corwin Press, 2001); Barbara M. Moskal and Jon A. Leydens, "Scoring Rubric Development: Validity and Reliability," *Practical Assessment, Research and Evaluation* 7, no. 10 (2000): n.p.

3

GETTING A GRIP

Phase 1—Research

In documentary we deal with the actual, and in one sense with the real. But the really real, if I may use that phrase, is something deeper than that. The only reality which counts in the end is the interpretation which is profound.

—John Grierson[1]

Grierson makes a good point about the nature and purpose of documentaries—that in the end, the director communicates an interpretation of the topic or issue of the film. To interpret within the documentary medium, and ultimately to be profound as Grierson suggests, students need to begin by developing a deep understanding of the person, issue, trend, or event under consideration. This process of building an interpretation begins with questions that *engage* students in the investigation of social phenomena.

So, before students begin considering their story arc, the aesthetic of their film, or the images that will compose the film's rough cut, students gather and weigh a variety of evidentiary sources and consider context, causal factors, interacting effects, and perspective. At the end of this phase, they construct a core argument that will be the foundation for the next two phases of the project, in which students apply an aesthetic lens to construct their final film interpretation.

These aren't necessarily natural processes for students and, for some, it may be the first time they encounter this type of thinking. While student-centered projects like documentary making are intended to empower students to build their own understanding, most students need structure and guidance for the inquiry process. In other words, there needs to be *soft and hard scaffolds* that the teacher employs to help guide the students' research.[2]

Soft scaffolds are those aids that teachers think of on the fly and in reaction to situation-specific issues that arise in the classroom. For example, if a student is reading a primary source document and is having difficulty determining the author or distinguishing the author's perspective, an astute teacher would step in and provide verbal context clues or make a connection to a similar exercise for a student to draw upon. Similarly, a well-timed question to a group of students such as "Do you have additional sources that corroborate or disconfirm the author's perspective?" can be instrumental in helping students' progress in their research.

Hard scaffolds are "static supports" that are planned by the teacher in advance of the learning experience.[3] In teaching students to research, most social studies teachers have developed their own hard scaffolds to assist students in developing questions and planning and conducting inquiries. For example, a teacher might use one of the helpful document analysis sheets developed by the Library of Congress (http://www.loc.gov/teachers/usingprimarysources/guides.html). In this chapter, you'll encounter a variety of scaffolds for the research process to help set your students up for success.

As a starting place, the research phase is broken into three primary components: (1) building background knowledge, (2) gathering sources and using evidence, and (3) developing the author's core argument. In each of these components, we take into account that most teachers have both time and technology constraints when conducting a multimedia project of this scope and complexity. Because of these limitations, suggestions are offered that might help make the research phase both efficient and effective, ultimately helping students to build a strong foundation for the next three phases of the process, in which the students move from argument (a strictly writing process) to interpretation (a documentary creation process).

BUILDING BACKGROUND KNOWLEDGE

Inquiry begins with the act of asking questions. To engage students over a sustained period of time, these questions need to be provocative, worth further exploration, and connect with the enduring understandings and essential concepts and content of the social studies disciplines. Grant and VanSledright define these as "big ideas" that help ground inquiry in "meaty, complex issues that are open to multiple perspectives and interpretations."[4]

Questions like "When is revolution justified?" or "What is the purpose of public schooling in a democracy?" are far more engaging than the simplistic comprehension questions often found in textbooks. These kinds of questions shift students away from gathering a collection of facts they string together to employing an investigatory lens with which all "facts" and evidence are vetted and considered according to the guiding question. In doing so, the research becomes purposeful, focused, and intellectually engaging.

Often, when teachers challenge their students to create documentaries without this type of guiding question, the students' work tends to resemble digital encyclopedia entries. For example, Kelly, a fifth-grade U.S. history teacher, began experimenting with two approaches to documentary making in consecutive years. In the first iteration (2005), she asked her students to create a documentary on a civil rights leader from the 1960s. Students chose iconic figures like Jackie Robinson, Martin Luther King Jr., and Rosa Parks and set out to create a biopic of their chosen person.[5]

Kelly experienced success in leading her first documentary project with students, but also identified significant challenges as well. Namely, the documentaries lacked an interpretive lens and "operated like expository reports of facts, names, and chronologies of events."[6] In the following transcript of a documentary made by a group of three students, this problem is seen more clearly:

Title of the Documentary: *The Life of Rosa Parks*
Rosa was born on February 4th, 1913 in Tuskegee, Alabama. She had to leave high school because she had to take care of her sick grandmother. Rosa married a man named Raymond Parks in 1932 who was a barber in Montgomery, Alabama. One day when Rosa got off work a white man got on the bus and there were no more seats. The bus driver told her to give up her seat because she is black. She refused. Later that day she was forced off the bus and arrested.

It is clear from this excerpt that the students had conducted research on Rosa Parks. It is equally clear, though, that there is very little synthesis or connection to the larger context of the civil rights movement. When reviewing the finished documentaries, Kelly realized that she did not provide the kind of guiding question that would move students beyond this expository approach. Accordingly, she changed the project the following year.

In the second iteration (2006), she focused again on the topic of civil rights, but employed guiding questions on historical myths or misconceptions, to help the students find an "angle" or voice. In the following transcript of a documentary made by a group of students, we see how this tweaking of the investigatory prompt changes the narrative to an interpretation rather than a report of someone else's information.

Title of the documentary: *Rosa Parks . . . Tired or Not?*
She was on a bus. The year was 1955. She was riding the bus home in Montgomery, Alabama when a bunch of white people got on and the bus driver asked her to give up her seat. She refused. "I was tired of giving in to white people," she later explained. This is a story of how Rosa changed history.

Many people believe that Rosa was just tired and didn't want to give up her seat. But the truth is that Rosa Parks knew and had planned what she did that day. She also knew that she could get in trouble with the law. She was planning this defining moment with the National Association for the Advancement of Colored People, the NAACP. One turning point occurred when, after Rosa's arrest, African Americans said they wouldn't ride the bus unless they could sit wherever they wanted. They called this a boycott led by Dr. Martin Luther King Jr.

In this example, the group of students spent time focusing on the myth that the teacher presented to them—*Rosa Parks gave up her seat as an impulse. She was just tired that day and had no idea what she was getting herself into.*

This example demonstrates that with a shift in focus, even young students can craft a more nuanced, insightful narrative. In this documentary, students ask a question and answer it using the evidence they gathered. Was Rosa Parks simply tired? Perhaps she was tired, but the students examined the historical record and found she was deeply involved in the activities of the NAACP well before the event and knew that the event wasn't necessarily spontaneous. Even more so, they went beyond the question and discussed the impact of her actions in igniting the Montgomery Bus Boycott.

Developing questions worth asking takes skill and practice. Working across grade and ability levels, teachers can successfully create the kinds of interesting questions necessary to anchor the documentary process in substantive and compelling inquiry. Some teachers choose to develop these guiding questions or big ideas for the students, and others have successfully worked alongside their students assisting them in creating their own.

In the C3 Framework, Dimension 1 defines *compelling questions* as overarching, provocative student-generated questions that give life to an inquiry or investigation. These questions deal with disputed concepts, unresolved issues, and contested ideas within and across the social studies disciplines, including civics, geography, economics. and history. Depending on the age of your students, the indicators within the framework suggest that these questions are collaboratively developed with the assistance of peers and adults. Compelling questions that frame an inquiry are the types of questions that could also effectively guide a documentary project.

For example, one ninth-grade geography teacher, Scott, used the five themes of geography to organize the documentary projects. Within the themes, he created questions about their hometown, Bardstown, Kentucky, that the students could investigate (table 3.1).

In another classroom documentary project, Katie, an advanced placement (AP) world history teacher, felt it would be a good experience for her students to create their own questions "especially because communicating a big idea is something that students, even those seniors, really struggle with."[7]

She structured a classroom discussion on the first day of the documentary project. Her students had just taken their AP exam, and they used all of this studying and preparation as a way to begin thinking about the themes and content they had covered over the year. The students brainstormed a variety of topics and then questions and voted on their top five. They used these five questions to organize their classroom documentary project.

After the project was completed, she was asked whether she would do anything differently. Katie seemed conflicted about having the students develop

Table 3.1.

Location	Place	Human/Environmental Interaction	Movement	Region
Where is Bardstown located? (longitude, latitude, hemispheres, continent, country, region, state, county...) Why is Bardstown located where it is? Why are Bardstown schools located where they are?	What is the climate like in Bardstown? (temperature, precipitation, seasons, climate type...) What kinds of physical features are in Bardstown? (mountains, rivers, knobs, lakes...) What are the people like in Bardstown? (occupations, traditions, clothing styles...) What types of plants and animals are found in Bardstown?	How do people use the land? (farming, herding, mining, industry...) How have people changed the land? What types of environmental pollutants are found in Bardstown? What kinds of resources exist there? (water, plants, minerals...) Why did people initially settle in Bardstown? (water, safety, food, natural beauty...)	What types of products are exported from Bardstown? Why would people move to Bardstown? (jobs, family, climate, religion...) Why would people leave Bardstown? (jobs, family, climate, religion...) Does Bardstown import goods from other places? If so, what and from where?	How is Bardstown similar to its neighbors? (traditions, language, foods, music, religion, festivals...) How is Bardstown unique? (traditions, language, foods, music, religion, festivals...)

their own questions and talked about the uncomfortable struggle that comes from letting go and giving over responsibility to the students:

> I think I might try to guide them toward those topics rather than let them pick. But at the same time, it was really nice to have them be really creative and come up with some really cool ideas, which is in the end, what they did come up with. I think there's just this tension, and maybe that's usual in the classroom, between, you know, the type A teacher who wants to guide it and letting the kids kind of navigate themselves. Because in the end, the film that they produced I think has a lot of really good things. And they thought a lot about the topic in kind of a sophisticated way. So I don't know, I guess there's just maybe a catch in there.[8]

These examples demonstrate the importance of substantive and interesting guiding questions, and that there is more than one way to approach this work. Whatever method you choose, the more engaging, thought-provoking, and "thorny" the question, the more interesting the documentaries will be.

In Edward Caron's (2005) article, "What Leads to the Fall of a Great Empire? Using Central Questions to Design Issues-Based History Units," he writes about the six criteria for effective questions to guide historical inquiry:

1. Does the question represent an important issue to historical and contemporary times?
2. Is the question debatable?
3. Does the question represent a reasonable amount of content?
4. Will the question hold the sustained interest of middle or high school students?
5. Is the question appropriate given the materials available?
6. Is the question challenging for the students you are teaching?

While these were certainly intended for the history teacher, with a little bit of tweaking, they could be used for geography, civics, and economics questions as well.

Other resources useful for developing compelling questions for historical inquiry include *Make Just One Change: Teach Students to Ask Their Own Questions* (Rothstein and Santana, 2011); *Teaching History with Big Ideas* (Grant and Gradwell, 2010); *Challenging History: Essential Questions in the*

Social Studies Classroom (Lattimer, 2008), and *Doing History: Investigating with Children in Elementary and Middle Schools* (Levstik and Barton, 2008).

GATHERING EVIDENCE

Documentary filmmakers go far beyond simply researching their topic. They work diligently to build a case for their interpretation by selecting supporting, persuasive evidence. This evidence might include interviews, images, data, correspondence, and any number of additional sources. Then, as the filmmaker tells her story through the film, she draws on this evidence to support, elaborate, and punctuate her interpretation.

In a recent short documentary, *Ken Burns: On Story*, by Sarah Klein and Tom Mason, available on the Web site for *Atlantic Monthly*, Burns even goes so far as to suggest that filmmakers draw on this evidence to manipulate the viewers so that they arrive at the same conclusion by the end of the film (video available at http://is.gd/gN5vYt). This illustrates the strategic and purposeful use of evidence in documentary making.

As students are building background knowledge, they should also gather evidence that they will use to support their emerging argument. This evidence can (and should) take the form of text information, data tables, images, interviews, videos, and any other kind of material that may help students construct their narrative and later, in the storyboard or production phases, help to illustrate the interpretation within the final documentary. To some degree, the topic and/or the guiding questions will inform the type of evidence the students will look for as they research.

For example, if the student is focused on creating a film about the impact of New Deal programs for reinvigorating the economy during the Great Depression, the student may search for historic data in different economic sectors during the 1930s and 1940s. This hard data could be augmented with oral history accounts of how these programs and policies impacted the lives of those who lived through this tumultuous time period. She might also conduct and record (audio or video) an interview with a family member or neighbor who lived through the Great Depression. Finally, she could draw on the vast image libraries developed by photographers at the time, including Lewis Hine and Dorothea Lange. Each of these forms of evidence should support the student's argument in a different, but complementary, way.

Interviews as Evidence

Student interviews with subjects who have experience or a perspective on the topic can be a powerful, vivid form of evidence. Documentary filmmakers routinely rely on this form of compelling and persuasive evidence in their own films. For example, eyewitnesses to an event, experts on a subject, and citizens expressing a concern all help to add validity and texture to a documentary.

One of the most impressive student documentaries using experts in the field to lend credibility to the director's argument is one made for the CSPAN film competition. Two high school students, Andy Locascio and Drew Precious, created an award-winning documentary titled "America Over Time" and used a variety of interviews to argue that the ability to amend the Constitution is the document's greatest strength. They seamlessly weave a variety of edited interview clips from an impressive list of subjects: Dr. Larry Sabato, political scientist, University of Virginia; Dr. Travis McDonald, historian, Poplar Forest; Holly Frazier, high school government teacher, Virginia; Representative Bob Goodlatte, U.S. House of Representatives, Virginia; and Dr. Virgil Wood, civil rights activist. You can view their video at http://www.youtube.com/watch?feature=player_embedded&v=I60Q4OsoG9o.

As Drew and Andy demonstrate, there is nothing wrong with aiming for top scholars and experts in the field. However, students can also think about doing what's called *vox pops*, or "voice of the people" interviews to add authenticity or additional perspective to a film. In this type of interview, students could ask a number of individuals the same question, and depending on their answers, use a montage sequence to demonstrate a diversity of opinion or homogeneity on an issue.

Regardless of the type of interview, it is important to instruct students on how to develop and ask questions of interview subjects. There are a number of strategies you may want to share with students, including the following list of tips and strategies for getting the most out of the interview. Students should be advised to:

1. Put the interviewee at ease by being at ease with the questions, the setting for the interview, and the equipment for recording. Students should arrive early for the interview, stake out a good spot, test the equipment, and review the questions before the interviewee arrives.

2. Give the subject instructions on how the interview will work. Students might share the questions in advance of the interview and/or walk the subject through the purpose of the film and the way in which the interview transcripts or video might be used.

3. Sequence the questions from close-ended questions (Where are you from? Where did you go to high school?) to open-ended questions (What do you feel are the most important elements of a strong education? How do you feel about the current national conversation around teacher evaluation?).

4. Ask the interviewee to elaborate on an answer if the student isn't getting what he or she needs in the interview. Using follow-up questions like "How did that make you feel?" "Why do you think that happened?" or "Talk some more about . . ." can prompt the subject to provide more detail to an initial answer.

5. Use verbal and nonverbal feedback to cue interviewee that he or she is providing the information and perspective sought for the film. Verbal feedback can be phrases like "Interesting," "No way!" "I can't imagine." Nonverbal feedback includes strong eye contact, inquisitive facial expressions, and affirming head nodding.

6. Listen to the subject. Good interviewing means listening to what the subject has to say and steering the interview to the film's goals.

7. Practice before the actual interview. Interview a parent, peer, friend, or sibling as a way to become comfortable with the interview process. Interviewing is a skill that takes time to master. Use it wisely by coming to the interview prepared.

When recording interviews through audio or video, the sound quality is key. It is essential to record an interview in a quiet space without significant background noise or echo. While students can capture sound directly through their smartphones or the built-in speakers on their tablets or laptops, it's often much better to use an external microphone for better quality. Even inexpensive microphones can make a big difference in sound quality.

If students are video recording their interviews, lighting and background choices are also very important. Simple backgrounds with good contrast with the subject are often the best choice. It's also best if there aren't distracting visual elements either in the subject's clothing (e.g., a shirt with a pattern or prominent logo or design) or in the background. It can be helpful to experiment with different light sources and angles to reduce deep shadows or glare. For more ideas on how to capture high-quality audio and video, refer to *Shut Up and Shoot Documentary Guide*, by Anthony Artis (2008), or *Directing the Documentary*, by Michael Rabiger (2009).

Working with an Archive

With the development of vast digital archives in the social studies disciplines, including the Library of Congress and U.S. Census Data, students have unprecedented access to a variety of forms of evidence that they might use in their films. Because many of these archives were not designed with K–12 students in mind, they can be quite difficult for students to navigate or find topical information or appropriate sources.

The Library of Congress has recently begun to organize and share primary source sets that offer small collections of documents (both text and images) that are very helpful. Unfortunately, for purposes of filmmaking, these kits often don't include the number and range of sources to provide student directors with the diversity and scope of evidence they need for their films. Teachers can assist students in this process by creating their own custom archives of documents, resources, and Web sites to make this process more streamlined.[9]

For example, in 2008, two fifth-grade teachers, Kim and Abby, designed a documentary project on the push and pull factors of Irish immigration to the United States in the 19th century. The teachers had only six instructional days to devote to the project, so time was of the essence. The teachers divided the class into four groups—each with the responsibility for developing one segment of a class film (e.g., Why did so many Irish come to America in the 1850s? Who were the Irish who immigrated? What did immigrants experience when they arrived in America? What was life like once the Irish immigrated to America?).

Kim and Abby wanted to make sure that the students considered a range of evidence and perspectives to build their understanding of the topic. They were concerned, however, that turning students loose on the Web or even in a digital archive would be quite time consuming for their fifth graders. To make the research phase more manageable for the students, the teachers created collections of research materials in advance that students could draw on to build their understanding and to support their emerging argument. These collections included data, newspaper articles, oral history accounts, and other forms of evidence. By doing this legwork ahead of time, the teachers developed an efficient *and* scaffolded research experience for their students.

The *Digital Docs in a Box* (http://www.digitaldocsinabox.org) Web site was developed as a resource site for classroom documentary projects. Here teachers and students can find examples of documentary tool kits that include texts, images, and audio/video related to a historic, anchoring question. These kits are expansive enough that students can select evidence to support a particular point of view related to the topic, but not so overwhelming as to be overwhelming.

Because documentary creation is a time-intensive project, most teachers have students begin with an archive or a collection of links they have created and branch out from there. This can be a pre-created collection like the primary source sets (http://www.loc.gov/teachers/classroommaterials/primarysourcesets/) offered by the Library of Congress or collections of links the teachers create and share using a tool like *Diigo* or *PortaPortal*.

With any of these approaches, however, beware of the school's firewall! In one project, the teacher painstakingly created link collections for a number of topics and found that nearly all the sites had been blocked by an over-zealous school firewall. It pays to check these out ahead of time to make sure that the resources your students will need are accessible on the network.

This creation of an archive for student research clearly has advantages and disadvantages. On the one hand, it makes the research process far more efficient in terms of class time. It also enables the teacher to "vet" the quality of the resources the students use in their research. In terms of copyright concerns, the teacher can also create collections of materials that are either in the public domain or have been released with a creative commons license to allow students to use them in their work (similar to the *Digital Docs in a Box* site). On the other hand, if part of what you want students to learn or practice in the documentary project is independent research skills, this approach clearly takes the onus off the students.

Internet Searches

To move students to independent research on the Internet, the teacher needs to think about a scope and sequence of research opportunities prior to the documentary project. This kind of strategic searching and collection of resources takes time and deliberate scaffolding. Your school library media specialist can be extremely helpful in thinking through or even co-planning this process.

For example, if students are beginning with a Google search, it can be very helpful to introduce them to the advanced search view. Students must do an initial keyword search, and then scroll to the bottom of the results page to find a link to advanced search. Once there, students can input an exact phrase to search for, specify a number of keywords, add keywords to exclude from their search, and even specify the reading level of the results. They can also specify the type of information they are searching for, including images and videos.

Some digital archives also include search tips and strategies for finding particular materials in the archive. For example, the Library of Congress offers a helpful page of strategies for finding primary sources in their collections (http://www.loc.gov/teachers/usingprimarysources/finding.html). However you structure an independent research experience, it is important to help students craft purposeful searches and to circulate among the students as they work to provide the necessary encouragement and redirection to keep them on track.

Structuring the Investigation

Of course, just pointing students in the right direction in terms of gathering evidence will not help them build effective arguments. It is essential that the teacher provides both hard and soft scaffolds to help the students be successful in the research process. Students need to consider the types and perspectives of the sources they gather.

In the process of analyzing the materials they consider, it is important that they consider both primary and secondary sources and differentiate between the two. They also need to consider the author of the sources and any potential bias or point of view embedded in the document. For example, if students are to examine the role of government subsidies in growing the economy, they would want to be somewhat skeptical of information published by the coal or corn industry—both heavily subsidized by the federal government.

Resources for Working with Evidence

While this is not a book about gathering sources and evaluating evidence, it is important to help students to gather a body of evidence that speaks to all sides of an issue and teach them to analyze each source individually and then collectively. Below are resources to assist teachers in helping students weigh and evaluate evidence:

In *What Does It Mean to Think Historically?* Andrews and Burke outline what they call the Five C's of Historical Thinking: Change over Time, Context, Causality, Contingency, and Complexity.[10] The goal of the Five C's is to give students and teachers a glimpse into how historians think. Furthermore, Andrews and Burke provide examples of how these Five C's might be implemented in authentic and meaningful ways in modern classrooms.

The Library of Congress (http://www.loc.gov/) provides teacher and student tools both for general analysis and the analysis of specific types of sources (e.g., photographs and prints, maps, sound recordings). It also provides guidance for teachers on how to use primary sources in the classroom. Similar to the Library of Congress, the National Archives (http://www.archives.gov/) provides suggestions for integrating primary sources into the classroom along with tools to help students analyze specific types of sources.

SCIM-C (http://www.historicalinquiry.com/scim/) provides a structure for interpreting historical sources that asks students to summarize, contextualize, infer, monitor, and corroborate using sample sources. Similarly, the DBQ Project (http://www.dbqproject.com/) provides a process for students to read and analyze sources as they prepare to write an essay answering a document-based question.

In addition, there is a wealth of books written with the idea of using historical inquiry with students, using primary sources to teach history. These are definitely worth a look:

- Jere E. Brophy and Bruce A. VanSledright, *Teaching and Learning History in Elementary Schools* (New York, NY: Teachers College Press, 1997).

- Linda S. Levstik and Keith C. Barton, *Doing History: Investigating with Children in Elementary and Middle Schools* (New York, NY: Routledge, 2011).
- Sam Wineburg, Daisy Martin, and Chauncey Monte-Sano, *Reading Like a Historian: Teaching Literacy in Middle and High School History Classrooms* (New York, NY: Teachers College Press, 2011).

One teacher, James, used one of these resources, the DBQ Project, to structure the research question, resources, and analysis during an eighth-grade documentary project he led on the causes of the Civil War. The DBQ Project brings together collections of documents around a historical question. The materials are created so that a wide range of students can access this type of exercise—not just the traditional AP student.

James utilized the DBQ on the causes of the Civil War to save time and because it offered a balanced array of evidence representing multiple sides of the issue. For each document in the collection, he had the students complete structured document analysis sheets to help them pull out key elements from the documents related to the focus of the project.

As students completed these document analysis guides, he encouraged them to put their notes and evidence in different "buckets" that connected with the guiding question. He guided his students to create categories related to economic issues, political issues, issues related to slavery, etc. Having students divide their notes and evidence in this way anchored their work in the guiding questions as well as helped them organize their notes as they progressed through the research process.

When it was time for the students to begin to flesh out their argument, they could easily access the pertinent information and evidence. As James demonstrates, the use of hard scaffolds was critical in structuring the students' inquiry and gathering of evidence within the instructional time constraints.

Additional Scaffolds for Evaluating and Using Evidence

Additional examples of how teachers might employ hard and soft scaffolds to assist students in the gathering evidence portion of their research are listed below. It may be helpful to think about some of these strategies as you begin to plan the research phase of your documentary project.

Suggested Hard Scaffolds:

- Structured 3×5 note card approach for note taking
- Guiding or supporting questions to narrow the scope of research
- Daily/periodic formal check of notes and sources

Suggested Soft Scaffolds:

- Modeling sourcing of documents (e.g., identify author, date, potential bias)
- Suggest specific resources that students might benefit from as they work
- Prompt students with questions to consider about a particular source

CITING SOURCES

As students build their background knowledge and identify evidence within their sources, it is important that they work to cite their sources by documenting the materials that they collect and then use within their documentary. This could take the form of source documentation note cards, notebook, or document using either a Web-based or paper-based system. You may choose to have them develop bibliographic citations for each source as they go, or at least note the Web site URL, book title, or other essential identification materials so that they can go back to these sources later for the full bibliographic information.

In many cases, as students are doing Web research, the teacher may just ask the students to copy and paste the URLs of the Web sites they use along with a brief descriptor of the source that they can come back to later. This has one limitation in that the students may not easily be able to match up their handwritten notes with a particular source. Another option would be for students to take their notes directly in the word processing document under each source URL. This will help to keep the notes and sources together.

Evernote is a free note-taking application online that can work very well for this kind of project. Students register for a free account for this Web-based service in which they can collect an unlimited number of notes. *Evernote* has a useful Web clipping tool in which students can select all or part of a particular Web site and create a clipping in the software. This brings in the selected page or text into *Evernote* as a new note. The service automatically appends the URL so that it is very easy for the students to go back to the original source for additional information or bibliographic entries. These notes can also be tagged with keywords. If, for example, students were doing research for a documentary on the constitutional convention, this software would allow students to categorize their research by adding tags of "political," "economic," or "personal" to note one or more categories that the note might fit into.

These source citations can be incorporated into the next phase of the process, Phase 2, documentary treatment, as students begin to build the outline for their film. This will enable you to quickly examine the kinds of evidence your students employ in supporting their interpretation. As the students then move to the storyboard phase, they can add citations into the credits, particularly for the images they select to use in the final film.

One point worth making in this chapter is that it can be difficult to include source information in the final films—software like iMovie and Microsoft Movie Maker weren't created for this type of classroom project, so the form and function of the credits section is difficult for capturing bibliographic information. Working with students early on in the process citing sources helps to not shortchange this important step in the research and production process.

Copyright and fair use can be tricky to navigate in the 21st-century classroom. While copyright law generally protects the rights holder of digital materials in much the same way as traditional printed materials, there are some conditions under which teachers and students can use copyrighted materials in their instruction and class projects. What's important to note at this point is that while students do have considerable latitude in using copyrighted materials (including images, documents, and video) in their films, it is still important that they document the source of the "raw material" they find so that they can provide proper attribution to the original creator.

DEVELOPING A CORE ARGUMENT

For students to make sense of their research, they must synthesize their understanding to develop a core argument for their film. In other words, before students begin thinking about which narrative structure is most appropriate or what images establish an appropriate mood and tone, they need to be clear about the argument they are making.

Both the Common Core State Standards for English Language Arts Standards and the C3 Framework place significant emphasis on encouraging students to make arguments by evaluating sources and using evidence. The early stages of the documentary process, if structured around evidence-based arguments, can help teachers meet these important, often state-mandated, benchmarks. Later in the process, students elaborate these emerging arguments by building an interpretation with narrative writing elements such as storytelling and imagery.

Ultimately, documentaries are intended to represent an interpretation by the writer/director. They are, in fact, intentionally presenting a point of view. Sometimes this point of view is subtle, as in most Ken Burns films. Burns has said, "In a sense I've made the same film over and over again. In all of them I've asked, 'Who are we as Americans?'"[11] While Burns explores the theme of American identity, other filmmakers are more provocative or explicit about their interpretive lens. Michael Moore hides nothing as he seeks to understand the cause(s) of gun violence in *Bowling for Columbine* or the impact of corporations on American society in *Capitalism: A Love Story*.

In contrast, the documentaries that grow out of classroom filmmaking often look more like digital encyclopedia or Wikipedia entries. They tend to resemble a collection of chronological events or isolated factoids about a person or event, as in the fifth-grade classroom examples from the Rosa Parks films. Another example comes from a pair of university students. In this adult-created example below, their film demonstrates that this digital encyclopedia entry approach isn't necessarily an issue of grade level, but more related to scaffolding the development process.

These two students created a documentary on the Montgomery Bus Boycott. From an aesthetic perspective, it was simply spectacular. But, when the smooth transitions, perfectly timed images, and period music were stripped away, we were left with a shallow, cursory narrative of the civil rights event. Here is an excerpt from the voiceover narration in the film:

> Some 90 years after the signing of the Emancipation Proclamation, Alabama was a place still plagued with segregation, discrimination, and Jim Crow laws, which implied African Americans belonged to a lesser race.

One such law required African American bus riders to give up their seat to any white that requested it. In December of 1955 Rosa Parks refused to do so. Later that day she was arrested. In response to her arrest the Montgomery Improvement Association was formed. At their first meeting they elected a little known reverend, Mr. Martin Luther King Jr., as their first president.

The MIA gathered their case and met with Montgomery City Councilmen; however, the all-white council would not budge on the bus segregation issue, and the Montgomery Bus Boycott began.

African Americans organized car pools, set up free ride systems, and did pretty much everything they could to avoid using the busses. One year later they prevailed, and the Montgomery Bus Boycott ends; however, this event sparked what is now known as the modern civil rights movement, a battle still being fought today.

While the last sentence could be interpreted as an argument (i.e., "this event sparked what is now known as the modern civil rights movement, a battle still being fought today"), at best, it is a relatively weak argument unsupported with evidence within the documentary. Instead, the narrative is a description of the events leading up to and following the Montgomery Bus Boycott. There are no historical sources or voices from the past that are brought alive through the medium, and the narrative certainly did not represent a nuanced interpretation of the past. Instead, it read like a textbook entry lacking any voice, texture, or nuance.

If these two students had used the phased approach to documentary making, they would have been pushed to define their core argument. Were they making the case that the Montgomery Bus Boycott was the seminal event of the 1960s civil rights movement? How would they contrast this event with others? What evidence had they uncovered that would make them come to that conclusion? Perhaps they would have liked to explore the legacy of the civil rights movement as they suggest in their last words (i.e., "a battle still being fought today"). With a clear *argument* or *interpretation*, they could have incorporated evidence to support their thesis and to organize their film accordingly.

In the Common Core State Standards for English Language Arts, developing arguments are an explicit outcome of the writing standards for History/ Social Science in grades 6–12. In the elementary grades, students are asked to interpret, but the architects of the standards cite different outcomes including "point of view" for grades 3–5 and "opinion" for grades K–2. In the C3 Framework, the writers explicitly use argumentation for secondary classrooms and point of view for grades K–5. It is important to note that in the end, no matter what you call it, K–12 students are asked to build an interpretation and to support it with evidence from a variety of sources. Of course, the sophistication of the argument matures as students matriculate through progressive grade bands.

Expressing a clear, compelling argument is an important formative "check" for the students. Is their argument well defined? Do they have evidence to support it? The simple template below offers students (in three to five sentences) the opportunity to define their argument explicitly using the following stem:

I/We argue that _____.
Because _____.

For example, using the Montgomery Bus Boycott example from above, a strong argument can be constructed with a thesis, organizing claims, and supporting evidence. A template for students to structure their argument can be found in Appendix B. The following is an example of a well-developed outlined argument that would come at the end of Phase 1:

I/We argue that the Montgomery Bus Boycott jump-started the Civil Rights Movement.

1. This event elevated Dr. Martin Luther King Jr. to the national stage.
   a. *New York Times*, "Negro Minister Convicted of Directing Bus Boycott" (March 22, 1956):
   http://www.tolerance.org/sites/default/files/documents/Minister_Convicted.pdf
   Document provides synopsis of the boycott, MLK's arrest and trial; quotes and photograph of MLK; illustrates public's admiration for MLK
   b. Associated Press, "Indictments Anticipated by Bus Boycott Leader" (February 15, 1956):

http://www.montgomeryboycott.com/indictments-anticipated-by-bus-boycott-leader/

Document identifies MLK as a leader; references MLK's discussions with various media outlets; mentions his need for personal protection.

2. This event generated substantial media coverage that introduced the civil rights movement to the general public.

   a. *Life* magazine, "African American women at meeting during bus boycott" (February 1956):

      http://images.google.com/hosted/life/13cd5afd22c7feed.html

   b. Herb Block cartoon in *The Washington Post*, "Tote dat barge! Lif' dat boycott! Ride dat bus!" (March 25, 1956):

      http://www.loc.gov/rr/print/swann/herblock/fruits.html

      Angry white man jumping up and down as black man walks away from bus stop.

   c. Newspaper archive shows that newspapers around the country were carrying stories about the boycott.

      http://www.montgomeryboycott.com/archived-articles/

   d. Associated Press, "President Gets Question on Montgomery Trials" (March 22, 1956):

      http://www.montgomeryboycott.com/president-gets-question-on-montgomery-trials/

      Not only is AP covering, but journalists are asking President Eisenhower about the boycott; clearly it's a big deal—he's being forced to deal more with civil rights issues.

3. This event showed that widespread public participation (civil disobedience) could lead to significant change.

   a. *New York Times*, "Negroes' Boycott Cripples Bus Line" (January 8, 1856):

      http://www.tolerance.org/sites/default/files/documents/Negroes_Boycott.pdf

      Two months in and bus company is still losing money. Document lists demands of boycotters.

   b. *New York Times*, "Bus Integration in Alabama Calm" (December 22, 1956):

http://www.tolerance.org/sites/default/files/documents/Bus_
Integration.pdf
Document outlines events of the first day of integration; mentions
that Supreme Court decision made this possible; includes a photograph of boycott leaders on the bus (including MLK); recognizes
MLK as a leader and includes quotes, one of which references the
value of their nonviolent approach.

If the students had been asked to use the argument template, the teacher
would have had an opportunity to check the students' argument before
the students moved on to transitioning the argument into the documentary pitch and the more fully elaborated documentary treatment described
fully in chapter 4. An additional completed core argument write-up can be
found in Appendix C.

ASSESSING THE RESEARCH PHASE

The foundation of an insightful and effective documentary is the content
focus for the work centered on the development of background knowledge,
gathering appropriate evidence, and constructing a core argument. To help
provide guidance for students and to help teachers assess student work at
this stage of the documentary production process, three dimensions of the
rubric correspond with this phase of the process (see table 3.2, and please
note that the full, reproducible rubric can be found in Appendix A). You
can, of course, add additional elements to the rubric, differentiating for your
own particular teaching context.

You may want to consider a variety of factors, including the age and
ability of your students as well as any additional skills that you would like
emphasize (e.g., independent researching skills) as you assign scores.

Teachers have found that the rubric serves a "gatekeeping" function
in the documentary process so that students can receive formal, formative
feedback before proceeding to Phase 2, documentary treatment. Because
the aesthetic parts of moviemaking are so motivating for students, moving to
the later phases becomes an incentive for getting the research to be accurate,
thorough, and ultimately insightful.

Table 3.2.

	Developing Basic Skills	Approaching Standard	At Standard	Exceeds Standard
Building background knowledge	Guiding question(s) were answered partially and/or with minor inaccuracies.	Guiding question(s) were answered or with minor inaccuracies.	Guiding question(s) were answered accurately and completely.	Guiding question(s) were answered accurately and completely in a comprehensive and nuanced way.
Developing an argument	Argument lacks focus or clarity.	Argument is focused and clear.	Argument is focused, clear and supported with evidence.	Argument is focused, clear, insightful, and supported with multiple sources of evidence.
Using evidence	Answers to research question(s) were not supported with evidence (e.g., data, images, quotations, etc.).	Answers to research question(s) were supported with only a few sources of evidence (e.g., data, images, quotations, etc.).	Answers to research question(s) were supported with a variety of evidence (e.g., data, images, quotations, etc.).	Answers to research question(s) were supported with a variety of evidence (e.g., data, images, quotations, etc.) representing multiple perspectives.

For example, if students turn in work that is questionable (e.g., approaching standard or developing basic skills), a teacher can direct them back to the evidence before moving on to the image selection or production aspects in the subsequent phases. James, the eighth-grade teacher mentioned earlier in the chapter, said this about using the rubric in this way:

> I utilized the project for really four different assessments along the way. The goal for the entire project was for students to learn the causes of the Civil War. By stopping after each of the four phases, I had ample opportunity to figure out if the students had learned the content. If they had not, there were a lot of different check points along the way for me to figure out if they knew the material—and if not, we could go back and address the issues. While it was a pretty long process, by the end, they had those categories down pretty well of what causes, what were the various factors, which led up to the Civil War, which was pretty critical. Even if their final film wouldn't win an Academy Award, students knew the material pretty well, which was really my primary concern.

CONCLUSION

Documentary filmmakers spend substantial time researching the topic of their films so that their final film interpretation is supported with evidence and relevant factual information. By structuring student research for a documentary project around engaging questions and challenging students to clearly outline their argument, with sound reasoning and supporting evidence, students have a strong foundation from which to layer techniques unique to the documentary film genre. In the next chapter on developing a documentary treatment, students will begin to develop the blueprint for their documentary narrative. Specifically, this phase challenges students to develop a "pitch" for their film and develop an outline of the content of their film by using storytelling techniques. It is in the next two phases that students move away from a familiar writing process (argument) to an authentic film experience (interpretation). So, dust off your director's chair, get a megaphone ready, and don't be afraid to don that beret.

NOTES

1. Ian Aitkin, Film and Reform: John Grierson and the Documentary Film Movement (New York, NY: Routledge, 1992), 106.

2. Thomas A. Brush and John W. Saye, "A Summary of Research Exploring Hard and Soft Scaffolding for Teachers and Students Using a Multimedia Supported Learning Environment," *Journal of Interactive Online Learning* [online serial] 1, no. 2 (2002).

3. Ibid., 2.

4. S. G. Grant and Bruce A. VanSledright, *Elementary Social Studies: Constructing a Powerful Approach to Learning* (Boston, MA: Houghton Mifflin, 2006), quoted in S. G. Grant and Jill Gradwell, eds., *Teaching History with Big Ideas: Cases of Ambitious Teaching* (Lanham, MD: Rowman & Littlefield, 2010): 3.

5. Kathy Swan, Mark Hofer, and Linda S. Levstik, "And Action! Students Collaborating in the Digital Directors Guild," *Social Studies and the Young Learner* 19, no. 4 (2007): 17–20.

6. Ibid., 18.

7. Katie Booth (teacher), interviewed by Kathy Swan, May 11, 2011.

8. Ibid.

9. Kathy Swan, Mark Hofer, and Linda S. Levstik, "And Action! Students Collaborating in the Digital Directors Guild," *Social Studies and the Young Learner* 19, no. 4 (2007): 17–20; Kathy Swan, Mark Hofer, and Gerry Swan, "Examining Authentic Intellectual Work with a Social Studies Digital Documentary Inquiry Project in a Mandated State-Testing Environment," *Journal of Digital Learning in Teacher Education* 27, no. 3 (2011): 115–122.

10. Thomas Andrews and Flannery Burke, "What Does It Mean to Think Historically?" *Perspectives* (2007). http://www.historians.org/perspectives/issues/2007/0701/0701tea2.cfm

11. "Ken Burns Has New Film On Mark Twain," *APNewsArchive.com*, last modified January 6, 2002, http://www.apnewsarchive.com/2002/Ken-Burns-Has-New-Film-on-Mark-Twain/id-3f117605e812b1404e000f93eaabdac3?SearchText=KEn%20Burns%20TWain;Display_

4

MAKING THE PITCH

Phase 2—Documentary Treatment

Your pitch is your first and best ticket in: it also turns out, a very good way to see if you really have a good film story. There are exceptions, but in general, if you can't pitch your story clearly and succinctly, it's likely that you don't yet have a handle on it.

—Sheila Bernard[1]

Once students complete their research in Phase 1, they begin to develop a documentary treatment. It is in this phase, students really start believing that they are making a documentary, not just writing a research paper. The classroom vernacular changes and so do the expectations. Students begin to talk of *story arc* and *pitching their films* and the social studies classroom transforms as busy directors and screenwriters work collaboratively to create a documentary treatment that will weave a character, issue, or event-driven narrative into the backbone of their films.

Because this development of a treatment is unique to filmmaking, this phase is often omitted or glossed over in classroom documentary work. However, it is critical in the development process, as this is the point at which students begin to establish the focus of their film, structure the narrative, and connect arguments they have developed and evidence they have collected in the research phase. Part of this work is an oral "pitch" to the teacher and/or the whole class in which the students create a brief synopsis—or "elevator speech"—about the film. As Bernard suggests, ". . . [I]f you can't pitch your story clearly and succinctly, it's likely you don't yet have a handle on it."[2]

In figure 4.1, the process of the documentary treatment is graphically represented. Essentially, there are two main steps, the pitch and the outline.

Although some of these terms may be unfamiliar to you, don't let the process scare you! In this chapter, there is a step-by-step guide for helping students to craft their documentary treatment and an explanation of how professional documentary filmmakers use this process to clarify their thinking as well as to seek funding to support their project. The process is adapted and streamlined for the social studies classroom, and a documentary treatment template for classroom use, as well as curricular examples to help you visualize the various steps, is provided. The chapter concludes by offering an assessment rubric that enables teachers to easily score the quality of the documentary treatment and to provide formative assessment feedback (see Appendix A for the complete assessment rubric).

Despite the complexity of this process, after reading this chapter you will be equipped with the language and understanding to effectively guide your students through this critical phase. In fact, students can complete the documentary treatment as they move through the suggested process below. By the end of this chapter, you will be searching the Web for "directors chair," "movie clapboard," and "megaphone" as you consider converting your classroom into a Hollywood studio.

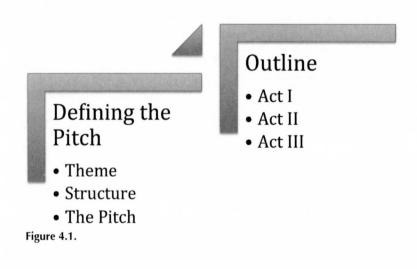

Defining the Pitch
- Theme
- Structure
- The Pitch

Outline
- Act I
- Act II
- Act III

Figure 4.1.

STEP 1—DEFINING THE PITCH

Prior to beginning work on a film, professional documentarians have to secure funding to begin their work. It is difficult, if not impossible, for a filmmaker to begin a project without financial support. This requires filmmakers to sell their films to producers before they've even begun production. They do this in the form of a "pitch" in which they articulate the focus and content of the film in a brief synopsis. The pitch has to convey the main idea or essence of the film in a way that is compelling. Essentially, without a clear, compelling, and persuasive pitch, there will be no film.

While sixth graders probably won't need to go to the Weinstein brothers to request 10 million dollars to support their class project, challenging them to create a pitch has great benefits nonetheless. By identifying a compelling angle for their argument or interpretation and clearly identifying the story they hope to tell through their film, you will be able to shift them from the conventions of writing traditional essays or papers to filmmaking and set them up for success in the storyboard and production phases.

This concept of defining a pitch is likely very different than anything students are typically asked to do in a social studies classroom. *And it's not easy.* Finding an interesting angle or story for the film was unfamiliar to the students we have worked with and thus required some thinking about how to help them make this important transition in the filmmaking process.

After leading an eighth-grade documentary project exploring the causes of the Civil War, James noted, "It was very difficult to get them out of the mindset of writing an essay, giving the reasons for the causes of the Civil War as opposed to we're going to present a story here. . . . I didn't realize until we got to the documentary treatment that was going to be a challenge for them and it was." Madi, a student in James's class, commented, "I think the hardest part was that, we had to pitch our whole entire idea in one sentence to start it off and try to get him to, like, quote 'buy' our movie. So like it was really hard to come up with that one sentence that would fit it because we didn't—we kind of had an idea what we were going to do but we didn't know completely, so it might change." She reflected later, "It made me feel like a director, and I really liked that."

To help teachers and students with this process, the following sequence of scaffolds will assist them in constructing the pitch:

1. Select an interesting theme;
2. Determine the narrative structure; and
3. Define the topic, story, and viewer question—or finalize the "pitch."

Each of these scaffolds will be illustrated through a curricular example below to make the sequence more concrete.

Selecting an Interesting Theme

To this point, students have identified their core argument and supporting evidence. Now, the teacher must help the students transition from argument to interpretation by challenging them to identify themes they have uncovered relative to the core argument they've selected.

A *theme* is a dominant, unifying, and/or compelling idea(s) that emerges from the research. Identifying themes is often difficult for students because it requires them to step back from the evidence and the days (or weeks) of research and determine what is most interesting or compelling about the person, issue, or event. Essentially they try to determine what would engage the audience and what story would be best suited to film. Themes could emerge from the selected evidence but could also be something student created as they think critically about the "why" of their topic. A particularly interesting quote from an interview or document, a provocative image, or an unexpected bit of data can all help a student to anchor or identify a theme.

Because students have grown up in a popular culture saturated with images and other visuals, one way to help them to find their focus could be through an exploration of images related to their topic. For example, if students are exploring the question "Was industrialization good or bad for Americans?" students who select an image of intolerable factory conditions would likely find a much different story than those who might select an image of a Model T juxtaposed with a horse-drawn carriage. Selecting these kind of iconic images can help students to begin with a compelling concept and inform the interpretation of their topic.

Once students have identified possible themes, they can then select the most interesting or compelling theme. Bernard writes that "[y]our pitch is the way to excite people about your project, which you need to do in order to get them to fund you, work with you, work for you, give you a broadcast slot, or distribute your film."[3] Again, students don't need to pitch their idea to the Weinstein brothers and so do not have to be overly provocative. However, they should consider the audience and ask themselves, "Of all these themes, which one would I want to watch a movie about?"

In the following curricular example, the students begin with their argument and brainstorm possible themes to their documentary.

Theme Identification Example: "Is Milk Really Good for You?"

This example stems from a civics/economics unit where the students were exploring citizenship and the role that individuals can play in affecting the common good. The teacher asked the students, "How can you [the student] impact the common good?" Students then selected a public health or safety issue, examined its societal and/or economic impact, and then took a stance or advocated a plan of action through a student-created documentary. Students viewed excerpts of similar documentaries including *Super Size Me* (about the perils of fast food), *Gasland* (about the issues surrounding fracking), and *Waiting for Superman* (exploring the issues in public schooling).

Among the topics students selected included climate change, "clean" coal, mountaintop removal, the legal driving age, and the legalization of marijuana. The group featured here focused on the milk industry, asking the question "Is milk really good for you?" They investigated the mass production of milk including the use of hormones and antibiotics in the production and whether cow's milk was actually good for humans.

After the group researched their topic using a variety of sources, they were asked to define their core argument and to summarize the evidence that supported their position:

We argue that cow's milk isn't good for you, especially if it is produced using antibiotics and hormones because:

1. Milk is difficult to digest; many people are lactose intolerant (e.g., approximately 30 million American adults have some amount of lactose intolerance by age 20) (National Institutes for Health [NIH, 2012]).

2. Humans are the only species that drinks another species's milk. Most animals stop drinking milk when they stop nursing (see T. Colin Campbell, The China Study, 2006).

3. Dairy food has been linked to cancer (see T. Colin Campbell, The China Study, 2006).

4. Leafy greens are a great source of calcium (see "Milk Matters" by National Institutes of Health, online).

5. Dairy cows are pumped full of hormones and antibiotics that are passed on to humans (see R. Schmid, *The Untold Story of Milk, Revised and Updated: The History, Politics and Science of Nature's Perfect Food: Raw Milk from Pasture-Fed Cows*, 2009).

6. Milk industry has a powerful lobby (National Dairy Council). Got Milk campaign cost 190 million dollars. See M. Nestle, Food lobbies, the food pyramid, and U.S. nutrition policy. *IHJS* 1993; 23(3): 483–496.

The teacher could have challenged the students about their controversial position, but they had thoroughly researched the issue and took a stance, thus making an argument with sound reasoning and supporting evidence and information. Once the students were able to do this, they were ready to begin thinking about their pitch.

Students in the "Is milk really good for you?" group generated the following possible themes as they began thinking about pitch:

- **Money:** The dairy industry has a strong political lobby, The National Dairy Council, that is well funded and well campaigned: "Got Milk?" There are clear profit motives, and the role of corporate industrial farming plays a dominant part in getting Americans to drink milk. Possible images and video clips include various "Got Milk?" television commercials and photos of executives in lavish office settings.

- **Tradition:** Milk is part of our American tradition (e.g., warm glass of milk before bed, Wisconsin the "cheese state," apple pie a la mode, etc.). Milk is an American staple and embedded in who we are as Americans. Possible images include happy milk drinkers from the 1940s and 1950s along with an old image of an Indy 500 race car driver celebrating his victory with a drink of milk.

- **Taste:** Milk tastes good (some say addictive "Casomorphins") and is in all sorts of food—from cheeseburgers to macaroni and cheese. Alternatives do not taste as good (e.g., soy, almond, flax, coconut milk), and they are more expensive. Possible images include desserts paired with a tall glass of milk.

Students in the "Is milk really good for you?" example chose the theme of money and to focus their interpretation on the "nefarious" role of corporate America in promoting healthy eating choices.

Determining the Narrative Structure

Once students identify their theme, they then begin to consider the narrative structure of the film. The narrative approach for documentaries can vary widely in terms of structure or focus. Three of the main film structures that are most applicable in social studies classrooms are character-driven, event-driven, or issue-driven films.

Character-driven films are quite common in both professional documentaries and student projects. When students develop a story around the personal history or journey of an individual, they tell their story through a single character. For example, students creating documentaries on the Underground Railroad might choose to tell their story through the eyes of Harriet Tubman or another "conductor." So while the topic is the Underground Railroad, the story would be character driven. For examples of character-driven films, see *Thatcher: The Making of Margaret* (http://www.chockadoc.com/thatcher-the-making-of-margaret/), *The Life of Barack Obama* (http://www.chockadoc.com/the-life-of-barack-obama/), and *Exploring Einstein: Life of a Genius* (http://www.chockadoc.com/exploring-einstein-life-of-a-genius/).

An *event-driven* documentary focuses primarily on a sequence of events or cause-and-effect elements to tell the story. For example, in tracing the move of the American colonists toward revolution in 1776, students might trace the story through a series of increasingly oppressive actions by the British government that seem to inevitably push the colonists toward revolution. For examples of event-driven films, see *The Crusades: Crescent and the Cross* (http://www.chockadoc.com/the-crusades-crescent-and-the-cross/), *Cold*

War (http://www.chockadoc.com/cold-war/), and *The Story of Computer Games* (http://www.chockadoc.com/the-story-of-computer-games/).

An *issue-driven* film explores a larger or more complex topic that may not easily be explored through the vehicle of an individual or a tidy series of chronological events. Our "Is milk really good for you?" example is one approach to an issue-driven narrative. For examples of issue-driven films, see *A Fall from Freedom* (http://www.chockadoc.com/a-fall-from-freedom/), *Aftermath: World Without Oil* (http://www.chockadoc.com/aftermath-world-without-oil/), and *Sprawling from Grace: The Consequences of Suburbanization* (http://www.chockadoc.com/sprawling-from-grace-the-consequences-of-suburbanization/).

By identifying the narrative structure of the film, students can then begin refining their pitch by transitioning their selected theme into a story structure for their film.

The Pitch: Defining the Theme, Story, and Viewer Question

Once students determine the theme and structure of their story, they can construct their pitch. The pitch is made up of three parts: the topic, the story (or narrative structure), and the question students are exploring. This is when students pull together the work of this chapter into a short elevator speech or a three- to five-sentence pitch.

The documentary treatment template found in Appendix D includes a prompt for students to help them frame their pitch. Just as with the argument, the students are asked to define their theme.
"This film is about _____."

Then, students are asked to identify the narrative structure they've selected along with why this structure will be most effective in telling the story.
"The film will be structured as a _____ narrative so that _____."

Lastly, students end the pitch with the question they want their audience to consider while watching their film.
"The question we want to explore is _____."

It is important to convey to students that a good pitch allows the viewer to participate in the outcome of the film and to urge the viewer to want to ask questions as a result of watching the film.

A bad pitch, on the other hand, tends to be matter of fact, doesn't draw the viewer in, and doesn't have an exciting angle or story to tell. If the pitch is a transcription of the argument and lacks a narrative structure or audience appeal, then it's back to the drawing board or to the screenplay.

Three curricular examples will demonstrate clear, strong pitches in each of the three primary narrative structures.

Example Pitch A: A Character-Driven Narrative About Lincoln

This film is about *challenging the notion of Lincoln as the great Emancipator. We trace Lincoln's positions prior to the Emancipation Proclamation in order to understand that while he was a great statesmen, he was also a politician. Ultimately, the viewer must decide whether Lincoln is worthy of the title "Great Emancipator."*

Example Pitch B: An Event-Driven Narrative About the American Revolution

This film is about *why the American colonists decided to revolt against the British crown in the 1770s. We will show how British policies in the 1760s and early 1770s incited the colonists to take up arms. In the end, the viewer will determine whether they were justified in this bold action.*

Example Pitch C: An Issue-Driven Narrative About "Is Milk Really Good for You?"

This film is about *challenging the belief that milk is good for you. We examine the health benefits of milk as well as the corporate farms and lobbyists who campaign for milk in our diets. Ultimately, the viewer must decide whether they should "get milk?"*

Teachers can be creative and have fun with this step by utilizing role-playing when students pitch their films. Some teachers have brought in principals, fellow teachers, and parents to create a Hollywood "boardroom" in which students have to sell their films to a panel of executive producers. Yes, there are props and theater involved (e.g., the executive team sitting in director's chairs or in front of the students) as students try to persuade the board to "green light" their films. This is an ideal opportunity to practice speaking and listening to others—explicit performance expectations within the C3 Framework and the Common Core State Standards for ELA/Literacy.

In both the C3 Framework and the Common Core ELA standards, students are asked to engage in collaborative conversations with diverse partners and to express their ideas clearly and persuasively. For example, in the C3 Framework, students are asked to use these foundational speaking and listening literacy skills in the service of an inquiry. Within Dimension 4, students across K–12 grade bands use writing, *visualizing* and speaking to collaboratively "present adaptations of arguments and explanations that feature *evocative* ideas and *perspectives* on issues and topics to reach a range of audiences and venues outside the classroom using print and oral technologies (e.g., posters, essays, letters, debates, speeches, reports) and digital technologies (e.g., Internet, social media, digital documentary)" (C3 Framework, D4.9–12.3).

In the Common Core ELA anchor standards for Speaking and Listening, students are asked to:

- Engage effectively in a range of collaborative discussions (one-on-one, in groups, and teacher led) with diverse partners on grade-level topics, texts, and issues, building on others' ideas and expressing their own clearly (CCSS.ELA-Literacy.SL.1)
- Present claims and findings, sequencing ideas logically, and using pertinent descriptions, facts, and details to accentuate main ideas or themes; use appropriate eye contact, adequate volume, and clear pronunciation (CCSS.ELA-Literacy.SL.4)
- Adapt speech to a variety of contexts and tasks, demonstrating command of formal English when indicated or appropriate (CCSS.ELA-Literacy.SL.6)

STEP 2—OUTLINING THE NARRATIVE

Once students have honed their pitch and developed and clearly defined their approach to telling the story, they can begin the outlining process.

The outline consists of the major elements of the narrative, including the supporting evidence they plan to include in their films. Bernard describes the outline as "a sketch of your film, written to expose its proposed structure and necessary elements."[4] She continues, "As written, the treatment should mirror the experience a viewer of your film will have, by specifying where and how the film opens, what moments it's driving toward, where it ends."[5] Essentially, the outline serves as the bridge between the pitch and the storyboard that will be discussed in the next chapter.

Like the development of the pitch, the outline is an extremely important formative assessment to gauge how students are progressing. While the pitch focuses on the big ideas, the outline reveals the detailed structure of the film. The outline is an opportunity for students to creatively organize their evidence and begin building an interpretation through the use of storytelling techniques. Just as the argument lays a strong foundation for the pitch and outline, a comprehensive and effective outline is equally helpful as students move on to the visual communication of their argument in the form of a storyboard (Phase 3) and finally the film (Phase 4).

There are, of course, multiple ways to structure a narrative. A quick Google search for "writing templates" or "writing scaffolds" produces literally millions of viable options. Experts in writing and English language arts teachers may suggest a number of different strategies to help students find their voice, build dramatic tension, and bring their characters and events to life. If you're looking for more concrete guidance on storytelling development for filmmaking in the classroom, Jason Ohler's book *Digital Storytelling in the Classroom* and Nikos Theokosakis's *The Director in the Classroom* both offer detailed explorations and elaborated approaches to help students in developing the story aspect of documentary filmmaking.[6]

Given the time constraints and content focus of most social studies classrooms, many teachers have found that a relatively simple approach focused on structuring the story around three acts, a literary device that is relatively easy to understand, provides some helpful guidance for students.

Act One—The Introduction

The first act comprises approximately the first quarter of the film's total run time. In the first act, the viewer is introduced to the central characters and/or events of the film. In many cases, the first act serves as an establishing shot and creates the context for the film. At the end of the first act, the filmmaker poses the question that the rest of the film will explore.

For example, the PBS Nova documentary, *Shackleton's Voyage of Endurance*, tells the story of Earnest Shackleton's 1914 expedition to cross the South Pole on foot (http://www.pbs.org/wgbh/nova/shackleton/).

In the first act, the director sets the stage by exploring the importance of exploration at the beginning of the 20th century, defining the goal of Shackleton's expedition, and introducing the team of explorers. The challenges the explorers will face are documented in detail. The first act ends as the explorers watch helplessly as their ship is crushed between two ice floes. The goal for the mission has changed from crossing the Antarctic continent to one of survival. Shackleton vows to save every life.

As students begin to think about their introductions, they should refer back to both the pitch and narrative structure they have identified. It is important they keep these ideas in mind, as different structures might be introduced according to whether it's a character-, issue-, or event-driven narrative. For example, in the Shackleton documentary (an example of a character-driven film), the introduction focuses primarily on the personal attributes of Shackleton and his team members. If the focus of the film had been more issue driven, the introduction might have focused on aspects of the story related to the role of nationalism and even the expansion of empires as the focal point for the story. By using the pitch as a guide, the students can better connect the focus for their introduction with the film's intention.

To help your students consider different ways to set the stage for their film in the introduction, you can provide them with the following questions to guide them:

- How will you draw the viewer into your film? What image and/or quote might you use as an anchor?
- How will you introduce your main character, topic, or issue?
- When will you begin your story?
  - For a character-driven film, will you begin at the end of a person's life? At the beginning? In the midst of a crisis?

○ For an issue-driven film, will you build toward a problem?

○ For an event-driven film, will you begin within the event? Start in quieter times and build toward crisis? Introduce the problem and then backtrack in the following acts toward context and cause?

- How will you introduce your question that you will explore in the film to the viewer?

Act Two—The Body

The second act of the film comprises about half of the run time of the film. In this section, the filmmaker gradually introduces evidence to provide an answer to the question introduced in act one. Ideally, the evidence should be sequenced and presented in a way that builds in action or intensity. By the end of act two, the filmmaker sets up some sort of resolution to be explored in act three.

In the Shackleton example, the unstated question is, "Will the group survive?" The body of film traces the challenges, obstacles, and hardships the explorers endure throughout the aborted attempt to reach the Pole and the later focus on survival. Rather than merely relaying a series of events, the filmmaker helps the viewers develop empathy and a rising sense of urgency and desperation as the film unfolds. For example, even as the men finally have the relative safety of Elephant Island in view, the current changes, and they are forced to remain on their small life rafts. Unfortunately, the remote island still offered no hope of rescue. Instead, they were forced to sail 800 miles in a reinforced lifeboat across the roughest seas on Earth to try to reach the South Georgia Islands. Finally, after 15 days at sea, the explorers sight land. They finally have to make an unprecedented crossing of South Georgia Island on foot to reach the whaling station there. This act ends as the men crest a ridge and hear a steam whistle signaling the end of the workday from the whaling station in the distance. Shackleton and his men would survive.

As students consider structuring the outline for the body of their film, they should begin by reviewing their research and argument. At the same time, they should make a careful review of the various forms of evidence they can use in the film, including quotations, documents, images, video, data, etc. They can then begin to organize their ideas for the body by considering the following prompts:

- What three to four points do you want to make in the body of the film that will help to answer the question you pose in the introduction?
- How would you sequence these (chronological, building action, etc.) in a way that helps your viewers explore the question?
- How can you represent these points by using various kinds of evidence you've collected?
- How will you set up the resolution or "answer" to your question?

Act Three—The Conclusion

Act three runs for approximately the final quarter of the total length of the film. In this act, the story comes to some sort of conclusion. This doesn't necessarily mean that all problems have been solved or that the hero finally prevails—the conclusion isn't necessarily a resolution. Rather the conclusion offers a clear answer to the question posed in the first act based on the evidence presented in the second act. In some cases, this leads to a new conflict; in other cases a new equilibrium is established. The key element of the conclusion is that it provides an answer to the guiding question and provides a satisfying sense of closure for the viewer.

In the Shackleton example, the conclusion focuses on a contemporary expedition of three mountaineers as they retrace Shackleton's route across South Georgia Island. The modern climbers discuss how difficult the trek was even with modern equipment and GPS navigation. The conclusion essentially underscores the great achievement of Shackleton and his men as a kind of homage to the explorer's spirit and the extraordinary courage Shackleton and his men displayed.

To help students determine how to conclude their films, they can consider the following questions:

- What thoughts do you want to leave your viewers with?
- Will you summarize your question and evidence? If so, how will you do this?
- What questions do you want to linger in the minds of the viewers?

- How will you bring resolution to your film (doesn't mean end—means closure) for the viewers?

While the documentary treatment development is complex, there is a template in Appendix D as well as a sample documentary treatment in Appendix E. This handout can help guide the process of developing a pitch and outline as well as provide a formative check for teachers before students move on to the storyboard outlined in chapter 5.

RUBRIC

The documentary treatment template can serve as a helpful formative assessment in the documentary film production process. The more feedback you can provide to help the students hone this detailed approach to the film, the more successful they will be when they move to the storyboard and production phases. Because of the complexity of this phase, there are multiple assessment points for teachers that are reflected in the assessment rubric below. The section of the rubric that corresponds to student work in this phase is divided into two sections. The first three dimensions or columns will help you to assess the pitch. The last two focus on the outline. See table 4.1, and Appendix A for the complete rubric.

You may choose to assess these dimensions individually as students complete each segment. Alternatively, you can use the documentary treatment template to assess these dimensions holistically at the end of this phase. Either way, be generous with your guidance and feedback of this stage of the work. The success of the final two stages hinges on a detailed and substantive documentary treatment.

CONCLUSION

In the documentary treatment phase, students develop a detailed and substantive vision for their films. While this process can be challenging and somewhat time consuming, this work is foundational in developing the big picture for their film. With a well-developed documentary treatment,

Table 4.1.

	Developing Basic Skills	Approaching Standard	At Standard	Exceeds Standard
Theme	The theme of the film is not clearly articulated.	The theme of the film is either not clearly articulated or does not fit well with the approach to the topic.	The theme of the film is clearly articulated and fits with the approach to the topic.	The theme of the film is clearly articulated and provides a compelling lens through which to approach the topic.
Structure	The structure is either not stated or does not fit well with the argument or theme.	The structure selected for the film might work, but another approach would be preferable.	The structure selected for the film is appropriate, given their argument and theme.	The structure selected is ideally suited for the focus of the film.
Pitch	The pitch either lacks clarity and/or provides only a limited sense of the purpose of the film.	The pitch is mostly clear and provides a sense of the purpose for the film, including the guiding question.	The pitch is clear and provides a detailed overview of the purpose for the film, including the guiding question.	The pitch is clear and provides a compelling purpose for the film.
Outlining the narrative	The outline of the film is unclear and/or not coherent.	The outline of the film lacks some detail and/or coherence.	The outline of the film is clear and coherent.	The outline of the film is clear and well-organized, creating a sense of rising action throughout.
Using evidence	The outline of the film includes minimal use of data, quotations, etc. from sources.	The outline of the film includes data, quotations, etc. from sources, but does not necessarily elaborate the narrative.	The outline of the film includes data, quotations, etc. from sources to elaborate the narrative.	The outline of the film describes a cogent use of data, quotations, etc. from sources to elaborate the narrative.

students will be positioned to elaborate their treatment to a storyboard as discussed in chapter 5. In storyboarding, students begin the process of translating their film from concept to completed product.

NOTES

1. Sheila Curran Bernard, Documentary Storytelling for Video and Filmmakers (Burlington, MA: Focal Press, 2004), 103.

2. Sheila Curran Bernard, *Documentary Storytelling for Video and Filmmakers* (Burlington, MA: Focal Press, 2004): 103.

3. Ibid.

4. Ibid., 115.

5. Ibid., 117.

6. Jason B. Ohler, *Digital Storytelling in the Classroom: New Media Pathways in Literacy, Learning, and Creativity* (Thousand Oaks, CA: Sage Press, 2013); Nikos Theodosakis, *Director in the Classroom: How Filmmaking Inspires Learning—Version 2.0*, 2nd ed. (Penticton, BC, Author, 2009).

5

FRAMING THE STORY

Phase 3—Storyboarding

A style is not a matter of camera angles or fancy footwork, it's an expression, an accurate expression of your particular opinion.

—Karel Reisz[1]

After reading through the first two phases of the documentary production process, it may have occurred to you that in following these steps, you could have your students develop a remarkable written essay. In fact, the kinds of thinking and decisions students make in the research and treatment phases translate well to a variety of different kinds of essays, papers, and reports. So what's different about a documentary than an essay or paper? Although many documentary films rely on voice-over narration to communicate their argument and story—and to a lesser extent on-screen text—filmmaking is inherently a visual medium. Even in an information-heavy documentary like *An Inconvenient Truth*, it's often the visuals that stick with us and create a lasting impression.

The nature of the visual medium communicates arguments and ideas in an entirely different way than written text. In fact, a director's argument or interpretation is often communicated much more powerfully in film through the use of rich and compelling visuals. For example, if a student were to write a paper on the impact of climate change, no matter how many astounding stories and relevant quotations they might include, the flyover footage of the melting glaciers gives the viewer a palpable sense of the severity of climate change in a much more visceral way. Similarly, in Ken Burns's documentary film *Jazz*, to hear not only the music from different performers but to also see interview clips of how they compose and perform their music lends a quality to the viewing experience that just wouldn't be possible in written text alone.

It may be tempting to assume that given how many movies students watch they have an inherent ability to produce their own films. However, while students are avid consumers of visual information in a variety of formats, they are not typically experienced in communicating through a visual medium. This is apparent in a number of studies in which students have significant and persistent difficulty in supporting their documentary narrative with compelling and even appropriate images.[2] For example, a group of seventh graders were developing a film on Harriet Tubman. For an inexplicable reason, an image of a cornfield kept popping up on screen. While it's true that Tubman grew up as a slave on a plantation, slaves did not grow corn, and she worked primarily in the master's house. In this case, the visual not only did not advance the narrative, the images used were both inappropriate and historically inaccurate.

Because students may not naturally know how to work within this visual medium, it is crucial to find ways to expose students to strategies and techniques to help them capitalize on the use of still images and video in their films. This shift from the typical written work that students most often complete in school to a visual medium is something that teachers need to carefully scaffold. Therefore, this chapter is divided into three sections. The first explores the image rough cut and how this process can help students to organize the visual elements for their films. The second focuses on helping students lend their voice to their work through narration and on-screen text elements. The third section focuses on the deliberate and careful selection of audio and visual effects to enhance their films. By the end of this chapter, you will have the tools to assist students in developing the blueprint for their films—the storyboard—that brings together the visuals, narration, and audio and video effects.

The different sections of this chapter will include examples from a student film project on the impact of the Dust Bowl in the 1930s. In addition to this anchoring example, you will find a series of codes that link to samples of other documentary films available online. These examples will provide further illustration of techniques and strategies that will help students to understand the power of visuals and other effects that add value to a documentarian's film interpretation.

At each point along the way, you will have opportunities to provide both formative and summative feedback before students continue on to the production phase. Try to avoid the temptation to skip these steps or to move too quickly through these phases. The storyboard is critical in helping students take advantage of the affordances of the visual medium and, like the other phases, will continue to build a strong foundation for the final production.

STEP ONE: THE IMAGE ROUGH CUT—
SHIFTING TO A VISUAL MEDIUM

During Phase 2, students built out their documentary treatment, including the pitch and outline. In developing the documentary treatment, students identified the core argument and interpretive lens for their film. The documentary treatment then becomes the compass and backbone of their film. The tendency at this point is for both teachers and students to want to shift immediately to writing a script for voice-over narration. This presents problems, however, in the production phase. If students shift from treatment to scriptwriting, visuals—the heart of a film—are relegated to a secondary priority. Students will then try to find images that fit their script rather than considering the role that images can play in helping to tell the story. This emphasis on the visual approach is not natural for many students (or teachers), so the documentary process includes strategies and techniques to help students linger in the visual.

It is in this phase that we must find ways to help students shift their thinking to this more visual mode so that images are paramount in developing the storyboard, or blueprint, for their films. Once visuals become part of the interpretive process, students can then write their scripts and consider how they might bring together on-screen visual elements with narration, music, sound, and other effects. This visual blueprint of the film is encompassed in the storyboard (see image below for thumbnail and reproducible storyboard in Appendix F).

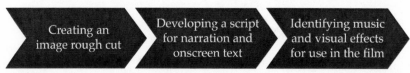

Figure 5.1.

As you'll see in the following examples, the storyboard should include a visual clue for what will be shown on the screen, along with corresponding narration text and references to visual effects (transitions, pan/zoom, camera angles), and any sound or music. To begin the storyboarding process, students should begin with an *image rough cut*.

What Is an Image Rough Cut?

Professional filmmakers often will create an *image rough cut* for segments of their films as a means to developing a visual narrative. In the image rough cut, the director sequences a series of images—hand drawn, photographs, or images in the time line view of a video editing software program—and presents this series of images to the production team, verbally explaining the flow of their story as they go.

This kind of rough cut allows the director and members of the crew to really focus on the visuals for the film. Once narration, effects, and music are added, it's difficult to really attend to the quality of the visuals. In practical terms, it also helps the production team to get a sense for the flow of their films and any gaps that might be present. Additionally, it helps them to gauge the quality of the visuals for communicating the interpretation of the film.

Tasking students with creating and presenting an image rough cut of their films is an invaluable exercise as they begin the development of their storyboard. It also provides a great opportunity to provide students with formative feedback relatively early on in the pre-production process.

To develop an image rough cut, students should begin by going back to their documentary pitch and outline they developed in chapter 4. By this point, they also will have collected a number of images and video segments they selected to include in their films. The creation and presentation of an image rough cut challenges students to bring together their outline of the film with the visuals.

The remainder of this section offers a step-by-step process to help the students create their image rough cuts, followed by a classroom example to illustrate the process in action. You will be introduced to a number of filmmaking terms and techniques, along with classroom exercises to help your students employ them in their work. It's important to note, however, that these tips are not equivalent to Filmmaking 301, or even 101. It may be more like Filmmaking 001. These techniques, however, will give you and your students some powerful, foundational strategies to "level up" your filmmaking work. A number of books are available that go into greater depth on the filmmaking process. While many are not written with the K–12 classroom in mind, they can still be helpful resources for the documentary aficionado. For more on filmmaking, please see:

- Nichols, B. (2001). *Introduction to Documentary.* Bloomington, IN: Indiana University Press.
- Theodosakis, N. (2001). *The Director in the Classroom: How Filmmaking Inspires Learning.* San Diego, CA: Tech4Learning Publishing.
- Ohler, J. (2008). *Digital Storytelling in the Classroom.* Thousand Oaks, CA: Corwin Press.

Organizing and Sequencing Images

By the end of this phase, students will complete the top row of the storyboard template (see figure 5.2).

To begin the image rough cut, students should use their documentary pitch and outline with the collection of images from the research phase. Don't forget video recorded interview footage that students may have captured. An image file of the first frame of the video can be used to represent the interview in the storyboard. The first step is to sequence the collected images according to the outline. This process can be done in a computer application like PowerPoint or MovieMaker/iMovie or with printed thumbnail

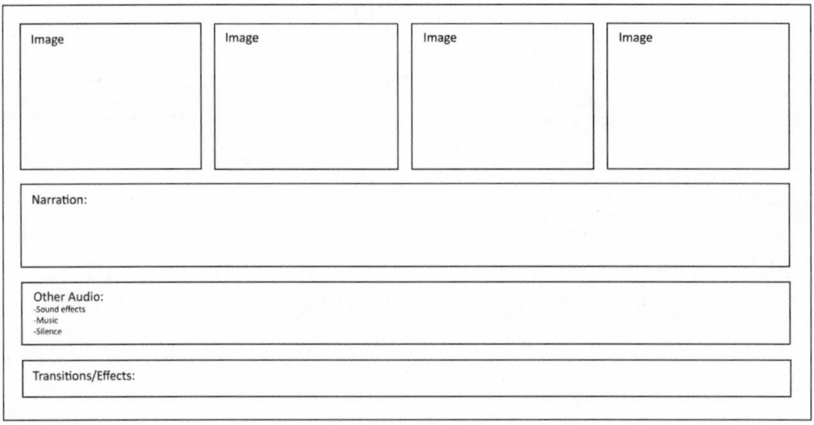

Figure 5.2.

images and a pair of scissors and glue. The important thing is for students to arrange the images in a way that helps them to tell their story visually. It is best to begin with just the introduction. When students consider the content for how they might introduce their films, they can comb through their stock images and identify those visuals that will help them set the stage and create the kind of tone they're after in their film.

For example, in a film focused on the impact of the Dust Bowl in the 1930s, the students wanted to give the viewer a sense of the scope and environmental impact of the dust storms on the prairies in the United States in what was called the "Dirty Thirties." They combed through almost 100 images they had collected and identified a series of images that provided the viewer with a sense of devastation that caused the forced emigration of hundreds of thousands of inhabitants. The images of a huge sand drift next to a house and a farmer digging sand away from fence posts hints at what these people might have experienced (see figures 5.3a and 5.3b).

In this high school student example on the Dust Bowl, students used Microsoft PowerPoint to sequence images on a series of slides—beginning to note techniques they might use and citation information. These students then presented their image rough cut to both the teacher and another group of students for both adult and peer feedback. This allowed them to articulate their story through the images, often coming up with narrative gaps on their

Figure 5.3a. Soil blown by "dust bowl" winds piled up in large drifts near Liberal, Kansas. Source: Digital ID: (intermediary roll film) fsa 8b27287. http://hdl.loc.gov/loc.pnp/fsa.8b27287. Reproduction Number: LC-USF34-002504-E DLC (b&w film nitrate neg.)

own as well as opportunities for visual storytelling. To see their image rough cut, visit http://www.youtube.com/watch?v=x3G2V6V6F8c.

In this process, even with the number of images this group had collected, it is inevitable that students will discover that they don't have enough, or the right kind, of images that they need to "visualize" their outline. This process tends to be recursive—meaning that students will need to move back and forth from image sequencing to image collecting to develop the first draft of their rough cut. Be sure to have the students cite their sources for each and every image using the system you developed in the research phase.

Figure 5.3b. Dust bowl farmer raising fence to keep it from being buried under drifting sand. Cimarron County, Oklahoma. Source: Digital ID: (intermediary roll film) fsa 8b38287 http://hdl.loc.gov/loc.pnp/fsa.8b38287. Reproduction Number: LC-USZ62-131312 DLC (b&w film copy neg. from print).

Using Images Persuasively

It's one thing to develop a coherent and comprehensive set of visual images to illustrate their outlines. Finding ways to arrange or present these images in a way that is interesting, compelling, and persuasive is quite another. Remember that the point of a documentary film is to communicate an interpretation of an event, issue, or person. This visual interpretation is where many students will face the most significant challenge of the filmmaking process. Fortunately, they will also enjoy the experience. To help them through this process, three strategies will help them create a visually interesting narrative: balancing the types of images utilized, employing strategic framing techniques, and developing montage sequences.

Balancing Different Types of Images

When students complete the first draft of the image rough cut, if they take a step back to consider the types of images they have selected and sequenced, they may notice typical patterns of image types. A number of image types can be used in a documentary film, including, but not limited to:

- portraits
- objects
- landscapes
- maps
- charts
- figures
- written sources (e.g., newspaper clips)

For character-driven documentaries, many students tend to rely primarily on photographed or painted portraits of the primary character. Of course, if students are able to interview the subject of their film, video footage would be a possibility. While they may have been produced at different stages of the subject's life, to the viewer, they tend not to be very visually interesting or all that different from one another. For an issue-driven documentary, they may realize they have used a number of charts, graphs, and figures throughout their film. Walking through from their rough cut with others allows them to consider this from the viewer's perspective. Students can also tally the number of images included of each type and think together about a range of images they would want to include in their films. A balance of different types of images, both in individual segments of the film and across the film as a whole, will provide visual interest and help keep the viewers engaged.

Image Framing Techniques

Another interesting way to help students understand the power of visuals in a film is to explore the ways in which images are framed. Just as photographers

Figure 5.4a. **Federal dead on the field of battle of first day, Gettysburg, Pennsylvania.** Source: Digital ID: (color film copy transparency) cph 3g01828 http://hdl.loc.gov/loc.pnp/cph.3g01828. Reproduction Number: LC-USZC4-1828 (color film copy transparency) LC-B8184-234 (b&w film copy neg.).

or painters carefully select what to include (or not) in their visual frame, filmmakers also determine what to emphasize or eliminate in an on-screen image. In some cases the visual power of an image comes from how it is framed on-screen. Take, for example, battlefield images used in Ken Burns's *Civil War*. To give the viewer a sense of the scale of casualties following a battle, Burns first uses a wide shot to take in a stretch of the line with corpses lining both sides. To provide a sense of the personal tragedy, however, Burns uses a close-up or even extreme close-up on an individual soldier lying on the battlefield (see figures 5.4a and 5.4b). Another example of this "Ken Burns effect" can be seen in his work, The Civil War. In the section focusing on the Gettysburg Address, Burns utilizes a number of different approaches to the technique (http://www.youtube.com/watch?v=qCXUbQ4JjXI).

Figure 5.4b.   Federal dead on the field of battle of first day, Gettysburg, Pennsylvania. Source: Digital ID: (color film copy transparency) cph 3g01828 http://hdl.loc. gov/loc.pnp/cph.3g01828. Reproduction Number: LC-USZC4-1828 (color film copy transparency) LC-B8184-234 (b&w film copy neg.).

In some cases, students will use the image as the photographer framed it. The framing of Dorothea Lange's *Migrant Mother* already captures a poignant moment from the Great Depression with significant emotional impact. In other cases, the students may want to "reframe" the image for use in a film. Going back to the battlefield example above, the students may find a high-resolution photo of a battle scene, but may want to crop the image for the film. This can be done either through photo editing software or sometimes even within the video editing software itself. To help students consider the characteristics of different types of shots, they can get started with four basic shot types: long shot, medium shot, close-up, extreme close-up (see figure 5.5).

Having students manipulate the framing of some of the images they have collected can be a great way for them to enhance the persuasive impact of their images. They may even use multiple ways to frame the same image for different use cases in the film. Manipulating the image framing

Shot Type	Purpose	Example
LS = long shot	The LS can be used to establish the setting. A wide shot of a factory floor will help to establish the scale of the factory.	
MS = medium shot	A MS brings the viewer into the scene. The viewer can begin to make out some detail to more effectively "read" the image.	
CU = close up	The CU focuses on a single point or subject that helps to establish intimacy or intensity. A CU may focus on a person's expression or action.	
XCU = extreme close up	An XCU focuses on extreme detail in an image – the eyes or a specific detail in a scene. This can be used to create drama visually.	

Figure 5.5. Image Source: Digital ID: (color digital file from b&w original print) nclc 01345 http://hdl.loc.gov/loc.pnp/nclc.01345. Reproduction Number: LC-DIG-nclc-01345 (color digital file from b&w original print), LC-USZ62-38459 (b&w film copy negative). Repository: Library of Congress Prints and Photographs Division Washington, DC, 20540 USA http://hdl.loc.gov/loc.pnp/pp.print.

can be difficult using printed copies of images. Importing the images into PowerPoint, however, enables students to crop an image with just a few clicks. As noted earlier, this can also be accomplished in many video editors as well. This may be one advantage to having students complete their rough cuts on the computer rather than in hard copy. Later in this chapter, we'll also see how other visual effects (e.g., panning and zooming) can also make for more persuasive and interesting visuals.

Developing Montage Sequences

A montage is a film editing technique in which the director develops a sequence of related images in quick succession. A montage of images can be used to represent the passing of time. For example, a series of images of newspaper front pages over many points in time from the civil rights movement can help the viewer to have a sense for the chronology of the struggle without using a lot of screen time.

A montage can also be used to illustrate a progression or sequence. This use of montage is more sophisticated and purposeful than a simple illustration of the passing of time. In the beginning of *Casablanca*, the director sets the stage with a montage alternating between a map and brief film clips from the route that many emigrants took to arrive in *Casablanca*, hoping to obtain exit visas to the Americas (http://www.youtube.com/watch?v=IU_raVGf87g). This montage, coupled with narration and music, suggests the desperation that many experienced on this trip. Another example of a montage can be seen in *Stanley Kubrick: A Life in Pictures* (http://www.tubechop.com/watch/1185081).

Another use of the montage is to juxtapose images that would not normally go together. This approach can help viewers to see a disconnect, injustice, or multiple perspectives on a topic. In a film on the causes of the Civil War, a group of eighth-grade students created a 30-second montage in which they juxtaposed the brutal and bucolic views of slavery leading up to the war (see figure 5.6). They used this montage to advance their interpretation that these fundamentally different views of slavery made conflict and eventual war between slaveholders and abolitionists inevitable.

Students can then present their image rough cut either to the class or just the teacher, talking through their story as the images appear onscreen. This is a great opportunity to provide formative feedback. Together, you can consider the following questions:

- Do the images fit?
- Are images compelling?
- How does it screen (e.g., too small of print, visually dull)?
- How is my audience reacting to individual and a series of images?
- Do they provide evidence, emphasis, or decoration?

Figure 5.6. Sources (l-r): http://hdl.loc.gov/loc.pnp/nclc.01345. http://hdl.loc.gov/loc.pnp/cph.3g01828. http://hdl.loc.gov/loc.pnp/cph.3g01828. http://hdl.loc.gov/loc.pnp/cph.3g01828.

- What other images might they consider?
- What are the gaps in their films at this point?

This feedback will most likely lead to another round of image collecting, re-sequencing, and possibly a second "screening" of the rough cut prior to beginning the development of the storyboard.

In all these ways, students can consider different approaches to conveying their interpretation visually. In creating and presenting their rough cuts, students can focus on these strategies for both development and feedback for their peers. Once their visual blueprint is in place, they can shift to thinking about how narration, music, other audio elements, and visual techniques can enhance their films.

STEP TWO: DEVELOPING A SCRIPT FOR NARRATION AND ON-SCREEN TEXT

In step two, we shift our focus to voice-over narration and on-screen text. This is the way in which students can both augment their visual interpretation and literally bring their own voice to the work. For this step, students will complete the second row in the storyboard template.

Where and When Do We Need Narration?

Because filmmaking is primarily a visual experience, enhanced through music and visual effects, the voice of the narrator can actually feel like an intrusion on the experience of the viewer. Like in a conversation, silence in a film can be uncomfortable for the director. So, while it's tempting to narrate every moment of a film, it's important to remind our students to embrace silence. Let the images tell the story. Narration should be used only *as necessary* to advance the interpretation of the film.

So when should narration be employed in a film? Narration can be very effective in helping to introduce the scene, subject, or theme. It can be used to provide information to the viewer that may not be obvious from the visuals alone. It can also be helpful to make connections between different segments of the film—making connections from one idea to the next.

To determine where narration or on-screen text is required, students should toggle back and forth between their outlines and image rough cuts. This may help students to identify portions of the film where the visuals need more explanation or when topics need more explicit connections. The students can begin to develop their scripts at these points.

It is important to note that one mistake in the construction of many storyboard templates is that they are often divided in a way that assumes that segments of narration are connected to single images and that there should be narration for every image. This unconsciously encourages the director to develop text for each image and also to limit the span of the narration to a single image. On the one hand, we don't necessarily want there to be narration for each image. Second, it may be more natural for a single bit of narration (perhaps even only 15–20 seconds) to span multiple images rather than with just one.

To work through this idea with students, you may want to engage them in an exercise like the one below. Students in the Dust Bowl group took four images and played with the following narration and timing of images. The one pictured in figure 5.7 was only one of the ways they could try breaking up the text, inserting silence and timing.

> Narration: *Confronted with this level of devastation, many individuals packed up and moved. [PAUSE] But where do you go? For most, that choice was California. Wave after wave of midwestern Dust Bowl refugees flooded into California.*

Students might also have explored the idea of creating a second pause after "But where do you go?" possibly inserting another image of a deso-

Figure 5.7.   Source: http://www.loc.gov/pictures/item/fsa1997026652/PP/

late road through the country. Talking through these possibilities with your students will help them to consider different ways to approach the narration.

It may seem that the storyboard is completed in a clean, linear process. In reality, many of these steps are more iterative in nature. In fact, it's likely that this process of developing a script for narration may help students identify the need for additional images and require them to go back to searching for images. They will then need to go back and find additional images. This may in turn lead to minor modifications in the script. Time constraints clearly help with the infinite regress of the work!

Scriptwriting Tips

Just as with the section on filmmaking, it's helpful to stop a moment here and remember that this book is intended for social studies teachers who are primarily responsible for social studies instruction subject matter. Screenwriting is definitely taking a right turn into another skill set not often familiar to the typical social studies teacher. Therefore, this section is intentionally brief, because a little advice can go a long way in shifting from a traditional written essay to a less familiar form, screenwriting. Below, you'll find four big ideas that may help you and your students as they begin actually writing their narration:

1. Use active voice wherever possible. For example, rather than saying, "The civil rights movement was advanced by students—black and white—across the South," a more active voice can be more effective: "Students—both white and black—advanced the civil rights movement."
2. Avoid long and complex sentences in narration. Scripts should be brief and easy to follow. A rule of thumb is that few sentences in a script should be longer than 20 words. One way to help keep the sentences short is limiting each sentence to one idea.
3. Match the tone of the project with the content of the narration. For a somber, serious topic, the narration should be more serious and formal. In a more upbeat project, a less formal, or even conversational

tone, might be more effective. (This big idea might belong in the *no-duh* category, but it's worth mentioning to students!)

4. Include brief directions in the script text to assist the narrator with how to read the script. One way that scriptwriting is different than writing a report or essay is that it is meant to be read aloud. The writer can include<pause>, <emphasis>, or<rising inflection> to help remind the narrator to read in a more engaging manner.

While these tips probably won't equip you to mentor the next Steven Soderbergh, these few tips will help to avoid some of the biggest screenwriting pitfalls.

STEP THREE: IDENTIFYING MUSIC AND VISUAL EFFECTS FOR USE IN THE FILM

At the Academy Awards, much of the attention and glory centers on the Best Actor, Best Actress, and Director awards. Although perhaps not as glamorous, a number of awards recognize the key role of music, visual effects, and sound in filmmaking. These aesthetic elements not only make the film more engaging and interesting to the viewer; they can also contribute to the director's core theme or interpretation. Who can forget, for example, the haunting and somber "Ashokan Farewell" used as the title theme in Ken Burns's *Civil War*? Careful selections of music and visual effects don't just "dress up" a film—they can contribute to the overall impact of the film.

In this phase, students will consider different music, sound, and visual effects that they can incorporate to enhance their films to complete the last two rows of the storyboard template.

It's a delicate balance here to encourage students to consider the possibilities without having them go overboard. In one film that a fifth grader produced on Harriet Tubman, for example, the opening montage of pleasant plantation images paired with gentle violin music is abruptly interrupted with the crack of a whip. This sound effect shifts the narrative to the harsh conditions endured by slaves. This single sound effect worked very well as a jarring element to signal a new direction. If, however, the director had strung together a number of effects throughout the film, they would undoubtedly lose their impact.

To help students consider the possibilities here, you may find it helpful for them to view excerpts from a few carefully selected documentary samples. In a relatively brief structured critique session, have students close their eyes and just listen to the documentaries for music, narration, and silence. As students view these examples, they should discuss effective and distracting uses of music, sound, and visual effects. Following this discussion, the class should devise their own set of rules, or guidelines, to inform their use of music, sound, and effects in their films. This document will provide a buffet-style list of possibilities for their films as well as a "check" against using these elements for their own sake.

At this point, students are equipped with examples and strategies to consider the inclusion of music, sound, and visual effects to help advance their interpretation. As they identify possible elements to include, they can note them on the final two columns on the storyboard template. At this point, they can begin to explore online to find the music and sound elements. Finding music and sound effects online can be challenging, however, depending on the particular focus for the elements. For example, finding historical period music can be much more difficult than finding basic instrumental music. Be sure to have the students document their sources as they go according to whatever guidelines you established in the research phase.

ASSESSING THE STORYBOARD

The storyboard is a critical step in the formative assessment process as students move toward the production of their films. At this stage, you should begin to have a picture of how students plan to produce their final films. You will be able to assess the degree to which the visual and audio elements work together to advance the students' interpretation guiding their films. The first two rows focus on the selection and persuasiveness of the images and the last two rows focus on the script (see table 5.1, and Appendix A for the complete rubric).

Table 5.1.

	Developing Basic Skills	Approaching Standard	At Standard	Exceeds Standard
Selecting imagery	Images selected are not high quality, not relevant, or varied.	Images selected are of high quality (i.e., not grainy or too much text), mostly relevant and are somewhat varied (e.g., people, places, objects).	Images selected are of high quality (i.e., not grainy or too much text), mostly relevant and are somewhat varied (e.g., people, places, objects).	Images selected are of high quality (i.e., not grainy or too much text), relevant and varied (e.g., people, places, objects).
Connecting imagery	Use of images and visual effects are not well connected with the narrative of the script.	Use of images and visual effects are mostly connected with the narrative of the script.	Use of images and visual effects connect with the narrative of the script.	Use of images and visual effects connect with the narrative and enrich the script.
Developing the script	Script is structured and organized according to the treatment but not developed.	Script is structured and organized according to the treatment and partially developed.	Script is structured and organized according to the treatment and adequately developed.	Script is structured and organized according to the treatment and fully developed with appropriate detail, evidence, and transitions.
Enhancing the narrative	Narrative does not use techniques (dialogue, description, use of first person effectively).	Narrative uses techniques (dialogue, description, use of first person) ineffectively.	Script effectively uses at least one technique (dialogue, description, use of first person) to develop experiences, events, and/or characters.	Script effectively uses a variety of techniques (dialogue, description, use of first person) to develop experiences, events, and/or characters.

You may choose to assess the storyboards as a whole once the students complete them. It might be more efficient, however, to assess at each major step of the process (organizing images, developing the script, and identifying visual and audio effects). Either way, it would be helpful to build in a gap of time between when the students complete the storyboard and when they begin the final production so that they can have time to edit and revise as needed. This recursive project can be both time consuming and somewhat frustrating for both teachers and students. If, however, students are able to address key concerns fully before moving on to the production phase, this part of the process will go much more smoothly.

CONCLUSION

In most schools time in the computer lab or with a laptop cart is a precious commodity. For this reason, making this lab time as efficient as possible is crucial. A well-developed (and revised) storyboard is an important aspect to this efficiency. This will help keep students focused on the key elements of their films and will make them (somewhat) less likely to get drawn in by the bells and whistles of the software. In the next phase of the process, production, you find strategies to assist students as they create their films along with logistical and classroom management strategies that will help you feel more confident and relaxed in the process.

NOTES

1. "101 Great Filmmaker Quotes," *Filmmaker IQ*, last modified July 7, 2011, http://filmmakeriq.com/2011/07/101-great-filmmaker-quotes/.

2. Mark Hofer and Kathleen Owings Swan, "Standards, Firewalls, and General Classroom Mayhem: Implementing Student-Centered Technology Projects in the Elementary Classroom," *Contemporary Issues in Technology and Social Studies Teacher Education* [online serial] 7, no. 2 (2007) reprinted with permission from original publisher, *Social Studies Research and Practice* [online serial] 1, no. 1 (2006).

6

QUIET ON THE SET!

Phase 4—Film Production

Editing feels almost like sculpting or a form of continuing the writing process.

—Sydney Pollack[1]

Now it's time for what you and your students have been waiting for (drumroll please): It's time to make a film! While students have certainly been thinking about the images, music selection, script, and effects, it is in this stage when students work within the documentary medium to bring their vision to life. In Phase 4, they determine whether their ideas work and what changes they need to make if their storyboard doesn't translate perfectly to film. As Pollack suggests, students continue the writing process, but within the documentary medium.

The success of the final film is predicated on a strong foundation laid out in Phases 1, 2, and 3. If students are clear on the story they want to tell, the questions they want their audience to consider, and the artistic tone and mood of the film, the changes they make in editing will likely be more meaningful and purposeful. And the good news: students are highly motivated in this stage and will work long hours and with great diligence to perfect their documentary. It is not uncommon for students to work together on the weekends at home (willingly) to finish their films. As the executive producer, it's time to enjoy the smiles and engagement that come in the final stages of production. But it's not quite time to sit back and enjoy the show—you have more work ahead helping bring the project to completion!

In this chapter, you guide your student teams to a strong finale by considering the filmmaking platform that is both accessible and functional for your classroom context and that meets the needs of your students. Additionally, you work to organize students into production teams so that their time in the computer lab or in front of a screen is efficient and productive. And finally, you assess their final products using the final phase of the rubric.

THE TECHNOLOGY DECISION—NOW IT IS ABOUT THE TECHNOLOGY!

Guiding a documentary project is much more about good pedagogy than the technology. At this point, though, it's important to make a deliberate decision about the video editing/production tool to use with your students. There are a number of options available for you to choose from, most of which are free. This section will help you to choose the one that fits your needs the best. Of course, you shouldn't make this decision in isolation. You'll also need to consider what you have available in your classroom and school, and what your technology team is able to support.

Software vs. Web-Based Tools

Until only a few years ago, only software tools were available to edit video. In fact, many of these tools were extremely expensive and complicated to learn. Fortunately, at this time we have a number of choices available. Some of these tools are software that is installed on the computer or device. More recently, however, developers have created tools that allow users to edit and produce videos online, completely in a Web browser. Each option has advantages and disadvantages.

Typically software-based tools like Microsoft Photo Story or Movie Maker and Apple iMovie include more features, are more flexible, and offer local file storage. For example, these tools offer multiple visual effects, captioning options, and export options that are not available with many Web-based tools. The downside with software-based tools, however, is that the project is confined to a single computer. In other words, if a group begins their project on laptop #3 from laptop cart #2, they have to continue throughout the entire process on the same computer. While projects can be saved on network drives and accessed on different computers, it often leads to technical difficulties that can impact student work.

Web-based options allow students to create, edit, and produce their films directly in the Web browser. This means that the students can work on their projects from any computer with a Web connection. Many Web-based tools also enable collaborative editing so that students on different computers (both at school and at home) can edit a project, sometimes even simultaneously. Finally, these tools make it very easy to share finished films through multiple services like YouTube, TeacherTube, or Vimeo. Unfortunately, these tools are often much more limited in features and exporting options. In addition, these tools can be difficult to use in a lab setting or in the classroom where Internet bandwidth is an issue.

Software-Based Video Editing Options

A number of software-based video editors are available, many of which are free. There are commercial software options available as well. One popular commercial option for Windows computers is Movie Plus, produced by Serif (http://www.serif.com/movieplus/). For Apple computers, Final Cut Pro is a powerful option (http://www.apple.com/finalcutpro/). These applications are expensive, however. So, if you are experimenting with filmmaking for the first time, you may want to start with one of the free tools and later upgrade to an application like Movie Plus.

It can be difficult to see how the tools stack up with one another. Table 6.1 will give you a sense of what you can do with each of the applications. Please see Appendix G for a more detailed breakdown of the features.

Table 6.1.

Application	Platform	Cost	Still Images	Video Clips	Transitions/ Effects	Audio Recording	Separate Audio Track	Audio Editing	Export Options
Movie Maker	Windows	Free	✔	✔	✔	✔	✔	✔	✔
Photo Story	Windows	Free	✔		✔	✔			✔
Movie Plus	Windows	??	✔	✔	✔	?	✔	?	✔
iMovie	Mac	Free	✔	✔	✔	✔	✔	✔	✔
Final Cut	Mac	$299	✔	✔	✔	✔	✔	✔	✔

Web-Based Video Editors

Since the development of Web 2.0 tools, a number of Web-based video editors have been developed. From simple video editing tools like those offered in YouTube to much more sophisticated offerings, teachers have a number of possibilities available. Like with the software-based tools, some of these options are free, while others are fee based. As a rule of thumb, the more features and flexibility offered, the more likely the service is subscription based. Table 6.2 overviews a few of the myriad possibilities of Web-based editors available. The first three are general tools that can be used to edit any kind of video footage. The last option, Primary Access, was designed specifically to support the kinds of documentary projects offered in this book. For a more detailed overview of features and options, please see Appendix G.

Table 6.2.

Web Application	Cost	Requires Flash	Still Images	Video Clips	Transitions/Effects	Audio Recording	Separate Audio	Audio Editing	Export Options
Pixorial	Free+	✔	✔	✔	✔	✔	✔	✔	✔
Weavly	Free	✔	✔	✔			✔	✔	
Wevideo	Free+	✔	✔	✔	✔	✔	✔	✔	✔
Primary Access	Free		✔		✔	✔		✔	✔

So, How Do I Decide?

You may be wondering at this point, which is the best option for your particular project? Again, it is important to check with your technology support staff to identify the range of options that are both available and reasonable for your classroom and school. Assuming you have a number of possibilities available, figure 6.1 tree may help you zero in on the best option.

Given the range of options available, it would be impossible to touch on all the variations and nuances with each video editing tool. Therefore, for simplicity's sake, assume using Movie Maker for the following directions, as this is probably the most commonly used tool in projects like this. Please

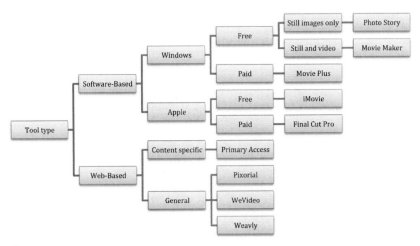

Figure 6.1.

note, though, that if you will use a different tool, it will be important to modify directions.

It is very helpful to create a sample film in the same format that you require of your students. This helps you to fully understand all of the technical challenges they may encounter along the way. If you are new to video editing, you may want to work with a technology support person or a more tech-savvy teacher in your school. If you take notes with rough spots you encounter, you can create a customized help sheet that can assist the students. If you can head off some of the challenges in this way, the production process will be both more efficient, and less stressful for you. In addition, a sample video can help to provide students a vision of the final product. You should be wary of students who may want to mimic the style of your video. You will need to assure them that they can be creative and develop their own vision for the film.

ENGAGING STUDENTS WITH THE FILMMAKING TECHNOLOGY

Once you have selected the software, it is time to guide students through the last phase of the documentary process. The good news is that often this is the most engaging phase—students enthusiastically experiment in the film medium as they sequence compelling images along a time line, crop and add effects to video they have captured, create the sound story of the film with effects, music and voice-overs, choose an effective color scheme with text slides and transitions, and so on. In other words, it's just plain fun to go digital and be unapologetically artistic in a social studies class. On the other hand, as with any curricular experience, there are important scaffolds to consider as most teachers will need to think about efficiency and classroom management in addition to moviemaking skills.

You may want to begin this stage of the documentary process by assigning roles within the collaborative groups that are making the film. As with any group project, it is important that students balance workload between members and that students' expertise is best leveraged. If students are working individually or in pairs, the following roles can still be helpful in outlining the key elements for this phase. Each role is intentionally mapped to the rubric for the film production phase. The following roles and descriptions provide structure for the major responsibilities during this phase of the project (see figures 6.2–6.6). Within each role, we have included responsibilities and "pro tips" when a student takes on the role of Director, Cinematographer, Audio Engineer, Talent, and Editor. There is a reproducible student role checklist available in Appendix H.

Director	The Director should be a student who has some level of natural authority/clout in the group. She is organized and proactively helps to solve problems. The Director oversees coordination of all roles; directly communicates with the teacher by providing updates on film production; guides the production team to complete their individual and collective responsibilities; makes sure that there is fidelity to the storyboard; organizes the screening of the rough cut film with the teacher; works with editor to incorporate suggestions after screening; and exports the final video file and submits it to the teacher. *Pro Tip for Director*: An important role that the Director plays in the film production is making sure that the team adheres to the storyboard created in the last phase. While some changes might be made during editing for visual impact, the Director ensures that the well-researched interpretation is not lost on the cutting room floor. Therefore, the Director should collaborate with the audio engineer, cinematographer and editor, and ask: How is the interpretation changing during the production process? What is lost and gained during production?

Figure 6.2.   iStock photo

 **Cinematographer**	The Cinematographer has an artistic flair and enjoys building the visual story of the film. In this capacity, she arranges images/video on the timeline while attending to their duration on screen; integrates visual effects (e.g., Ken Burns effect, film grain, etc.); creates title and text slides; and prepares and imports credits slides. *Pro Tip for Cinematographer:* While most moviemaking software allows the student to create text slides and credits within the software, most platforms are not flexible enough to accommodate the detailed kinds of citations that you may require. For more flexibility, students can create text slides in Microsoft *PowerPoint* and then import the slides as images into the film.

Figure 6.3. iStock photo

 **Talent**	The Talent should be someone who likes to perform. He is primarily responsible for the narration of the film, either as the primary narrator or coordinator of the narrating voices. The Talent encourages students to be creative and to find their own voice in the medium; coordinates practice readings before recording for the film; matches tone of recording with mood of the film; provides peer feedback on the recordings; and organizes audio files for import (if recorded outside of the moviemaking platform). *Pro Tips for the Talent:* Rehearse. Rehearse. Rehearse. You would be surprised how difficult it is to have students read the script clearly and with inflection. Perhaps it stems from a stereotype of documentary films—in order to take on a serious topic, students often read with a grave, monotone voice. By running through and recording a "table read" students can hear and critique exactly how they bring the script to life. As they listen to this initial recording, the Talent can consider vocal variety, inflection, emphasis, volume and tone to inform how they record the narration. Students should be encouraged to try different approaches during the rehearsal process—the great thing about digital recording is that the only limit on the amount of takes is when the bell rings for the next class or when you decide it's time for students to move on!

Figure 6.4. iStock photo

 **Audio Engineer**	The Audio Engineer should have an *ear* for film and some technical expertise with the documentary platform you choose. He will be responsible for importing audio narration files into appropriate places on the timeline; integrating additional audio effects (fade in and fade out); synchronizing music and other audio files on timeline; making sure volume levels are consistent across the film; and working with Cinematographer on timing of images and sound. *Pro Tip for the Audio Engineer:* The audio engineer should not be a "hammer in search of a nail". The use of silence in a film is often an underused technique—a strategic pregnant pause in the audio track of the film can be often as powerful as the soundtrack to the documentary.

Figure 6.5. iStock photo

	The Editor should be the most technology savvy member of the group. She is responsible for the "micro edits" as the pieces come together. She also completes final edits as suggested by other production team members. While the Cinematographer and Audio Engineer are presumably working together, the Editor does the final work of aligning images, audio, and sounds according to storyboard; ensuring that the overall film has impact and is cohesive; working with the Director to produce a Rough Cut of the film; and assisting the Director with the additional edits prior to final film submission.
  Editor	*Pro Tip for the Editor:* The Editor should push for a teacher and/or peer review of the film's rough cut. The "rough cut" is simply a rendering of the film that is viewed by others before final editing. This viewing can be done as a class, which in many ways is ideal. Students are able to see each other's films and instead of saying, "We should have…could have…would have had we known", they can apply others' suggestions and ideas into their film before they hand it in for a final grade and prepare for the screening.

Figure 6.6.   iStock photo

WHAT TO EXPECT WHEN YOU'RE EXPECTING MULTIPLE CLASSROOM FILM PROJECTS

It's important in managing documentary projects to temper expectations. Once we had a professional documentarian view a set of fifth grade films to gather advice on how to better structure future documentary projects. Unfortunately, despite the fact that the creators were ten and eleven-year olds, he simply couldn't get past all of the technical issues that seemed rampant throughout the films. He was viewing the films through the eyes and experience of a career in filmmaking. It is important to remember that students have little, if any, experience creating films.

A consideration when doing this kind of work with students is that they do not have the expertise, budget, or time of Ken Burns. This is probably obvious to you but it is important to recognize. Perhaps because documentary projects are created to be shared with others, viewers take on a more critical eye. Some students have a natural talent or instinct with this type of work and can produce impressive documentary films. An example of this is high school student Josh Stokes, who was the 2013 C-SPAN Student Cam Student Documentary Competition Grand Prize Winner for his film *Unemployment in America* (http://studentcam.viddler.com/videos/watch.php?id=1dc69c8).

While some student films will win national awards like this one, most will not be nearly as polished. But often what students can represent in a final film isn't a perfect representation of what they know or learned in the project. Grant calls this the representation dilemma.[2] According to Grant, the representation dilemma has several dimensions including: (a) the "fluidity of student ideas" or students' coherence or consistency of ideas; (b) the ability of students, particularly adolescents, to communicate their understanding through oral or written means; and (c) the "context in which students are asked to represent their historical knowledge or understandings."[3] In other words, trying to assess what students know is pretty tricky in a multistage, multimodal project like this one—particularly if this is a student's first experience making a documentary.

Implementing the work through the four-phase approach with a particular emphasis on formative assessment or checkpoints helps capture the students' growth throughout the project and takes pressure off this final stage that requires a great deal of technical expertise. Students who are new to the medium might find it particularly challenging representing what they know in the form of a documentary, just like a first experience in writing can often obscure what students know and understand about a particular topic. Measuring student skill development and knowledge always has limitations but striving to capture the layers of understanding inherent in the documentary process should be the goal.

Assessing Film Production

The last phase of the rubric focuses on the elements of the final film. Students are assessed on the visual and audio structure of the documentary and the ways in which those components contribute to the overall impact of the film. These aspects of film might feel a bit subjective. As a form of art, this is un-avoidable. Remember, though, that you have already assessed many objective aspects of the process. However, as you become more acquainted with the medium, what it can evoke, how it can be used effectively, and what can be expected at grade level, you will feel more comfortable in assessing this aspect of the work. Think about the first time you gave students a grade on an essay, or a poster project, or a debate. As you already know, assessing students is never easy, but over time, and with more experience in film, you will understand that

Table 6.3. Phase Four: Film Production

	Developing Basic Skills	Approaching Standard	At Standard	Exceeds Standard
Using Visual Effects	Use of images and visual effects (e.g., panning, zooming, transitions, text captions) is not well connected with the narrative of the film.	Use of images and visual effects (e.g., panning, zooming, transitions, text captions) is mostly connected with the narrative of the film.	Use of visual effects (e.g., panning, zooming, transitions, text captions) is well-connected with the narrative of the film.	Use of images and visual effects (e.g., panning, zooming, transitions, text captions) enhances/enriches the film.
Voice/Sound Communication	Narration (volume, diction, fluency, flow, inflection) and use of audio (music, effects, silence) are not well connected to the tone, style, and theme of the film.	Narration (volume, diction, fluency, flow, inflection) and use of audio (music, effects, silence) connects with the tone, style, and theme of the film.	Narration (volume, diction, fluency, flow, inflection) and use of audio (music, effects, silence) contributes to the tone, style, and theme of the film.	Narration (volume, diction, fluency, flow, inflection) and use of audio (music, effects, silence) are integral in telling the story.
Final Editing	The final editing of the film (timing of narration and images, pacing, titles and credits) is not acceptable and/or detracts from the story.	The final editing of the film (timing of narration and images, pacing, titles and credits) is acceptable and does not detract from the story.	The final editing of the film (timing of narration and images, pacing, titles and credits) is mostly polished.	The final editing of the film (timing of narration and images, pacing, titles and credits) is polished and enhances the story.
Overall Impact of the Film	The overall impact of the film is limited. The film does not adequately portray the interpretation of the film.	The overall impact of the film is mostly positive. The film adequately portrays the interpretation of the film.	The overall impact of the film is positive. The film effectively portrays the interpretation of the film.	The overall impact of the film is powerful. The film effectively portrays the interpretation of the film.

there are conventions that exist in every form of expression from sculpture to poetry to film—and you will learn how to provide feedback accordingly. See table 6.3, and Appendix A for the complete rubric.

One thing that can be challenging and a little frustrating for teachers leading a documentary project is that sometimes you may not always understand the choices they make or even see full evidence of what they understand about the topic. One clever and fun way to gain a better understanding of the students' perspective on the film is through the creation of a "director's commentary." Just like with a feature film, students can record an audio commentary over their final film to discuss their artistic choices and insights into the work. To do this, students just import their final film back into the video editor and add on a narration track across the whole movie. It takes only a little extra time, but it can be a good exercise for the students and enlightening for the teacher.

CONCLUSION

At the end of this phase, students should have completed their films. And while the hard work is finished, one important step remains—to enable your students to share their work beyond the four walls of the classroom. The next chapter offers tips for hosting a classroom or school-wide film festival as well as additional opportunities for students to enter filmmaking competitions. In addition to these opportunities, the next chapter also offers guidance for hosting video files online and navigating the ambiguous waters of copyright law.

NOTES

1. "Biography for Sydney Pollack," IMDb.com, accessed August 22, 2013, http://www.imdb.com/name/nm0001628/bio.

2. S. G. Grant, "Understanding What Children Know About History: Exploring the Representation and Testing Dilemmas," *Social Studies Research and Practice* 2, no. 2 (2007): 196–208.

3. Ibid., 197.

7

PREMIERING THE FILMS

Sharing Student Work

We are born into a box of time and space. We use words and communication to break out of it and to reach out to others.

—Roger Ebert[1]

No one enjoyed a film premiere more than the legendary film critic Roger Ebert. Using his iconic thumbs up and down metric with longtime colleague, Gene Siskel, they gave audiences a glimpse into the art of film conversation and critique in their weekly show *At the Movies*. Often disagreeing in their assessments, Siskel and Ebert knew that film is ultimately a provocative medium intended to be consumed and discussed within a community. In Ebert's words, "We are born into a box of time and space. We use words and communication to break out of it and to reach out to others."

Ultimately, the purpose of documentary film is to provoke others to action—either in the way they view the topic or through direct community action. The documentary project "Got Milk?" featured in chapter 4 serves as a good example of a community taking informed action. The student directors of this film shared their final product with the school community, and while milk remained a staple at the elementary lunch table, the principal was so persuaded by the argument in the film, she insisted that all milk coming into the school needed to be organic.

Not all film projects should or will have this kind of impact. But educational research demonstrates that when students perceive their work as having value beyond the walls of the classroom, they spend more time, complete more revisions, and take greater pride in their work.[2] You would be hard pressed to find a book or article on K–12 filmmaking that doesn't make a similar argument. The technology is certainly motivating for students, but so too is the opportunity to extend beyond the four walls of the classroom and share their hard work with a wider community.

In this chapter, you will learn how to share your students' work in a variety of ways. This will help you to shift your students' perspectives from being consumers to producers of media by considering copyright concerns and ethical issues in this medium. You will be able to identify the best online sharing service to select, relative to your school's and division's policies. Finally, you will identify opportunities to create a film festival in your class or school to both celebrate and disseminate your students' work. A number of student film festivals also offer both incentives and motivation for student-produced films.

A TEACHABLE MOMENT—MEDIA LITERACY, COPYRIGHT, AND PRIVACY ISSUES IN FILM

While perhaps not the most exciting part of leading a documentary project, discussing with students some of the big picture issues related to copyright and privacy can be a powerful "teachable moment" for students. Up to this point, the majority of students in your class have been either primarily or completely consumers of digital media. For many, this will be their first foray into creating content that others will view and enjoy. Consequently, many students probably haven't given much thought to some of the ethical issues surrounding digital media. As a step in the process of sharing their work with a wider audience, this can be a great opportunity to explore some media literacy concepts with your class.

A Copyright Primer

This section will introduce you to the genesis, interpretations, and limitations related to copyright. This is not meant to be exhaustive and is clearly not legal advice. However, it will help to create a context within which you can consider using copyrighted materials in the context of creating films. For a more detailed look at copyright in the classroom, be sure to pick up a copy of *Copyright Clarity: How Fair Use Supports Digital Learning*, by Renee Hobbs.[3] It is a very interesting, helpful, and practical read for teachers concerned about copyright issues in the classroom.

Copyright to students (and many teachers) can seem like a restrictive and stifling set of complex rules and regulations. In fact, this is how copyright is often addressed in school policies—essentially a list of all the things that you can't or shouldn't do related to copyrighted work found online. In actuality, though, copyright was designed to protect the rights of content creators while recognizing the social benefits of publication and sharing. It was designed as a way to ensure that writers, artists, inventors, and others who share their work are both credited for their contribution and compensated fairly for the time, effort, blood, sweat, and tears that go into creative work. As students shift into the role of being a creator of content, they may be more open to understanding and really considering copyright—and perhaps more likely to abide by the rules as well.

First, it may be helpful to define copyright. Renee Hobbs, media literacy guru and author of *Copyright Clarity*, offers the following definition: "Copyright is the owner's legal right to reproduce, display, transmit, or modify work they have created. It's a type of author right. Patent law protects the works of inventors. Together, the works of authors and inventors are called intellectual property."[4] The fair use doctrine, however, provides exceptions to copyright law to allow limited use of copyrighted materials without the permission of the copyright holder. Hobbs notes, "At the heart of copyright law, the doctrine of fair use states that people have a right to use copyrighted materials freely, without payment or permission, for purposes such as criticism, comment, news reporting, teaching, scholarship, and research."[5] These exceptions provide powerful opportunities for teachers and students to use copyrighted works in the context of teaching and learning.

Section 107 of Title 17 of the U.S. Code outlines four factors that should be considered to determine whether a use of copyrighted material could be considered fair use:

1. The purpose and character of the use, including whether such use is of commercial nature or is for nonprofit educational purposes

2. The nature of the copyrighted work
3. The amount and substantiality of the portion used in relation to the copyrighted work as a whole
4. The effect of the use upon the potential market for, or value of, the copyrighted work[6]

Many educators have adopted this four-factor test as a key determinant that should guide school policy. Many media literacy experts, however, see this "checklist" approach as unnecessarily limiting. In fact, Carrie Russell of the American Library Association states, "Fair use cannot be reduced to a checklist. Fair use requires that people think.[7] Hobbs argues, "In recent years, courts have recognized that when a user of copyrighted materials adds value to, or repurposes materials for a use different from that for which it was originally intended, it will likely be considered fair use. Fair use embraces the modification of existing content if it is placed in new context."[8]

While copyright lawyers disagree about the specific parameters of fair use, one element is particularly important for teachers in filmmaking—transformation. The more that a teacher or students transform the copyrighted material in their use, the more likely this would be considered fair use. So, for example, a series of broadsides posted during World War II urging citizens to support the war effort were originally produced as a means to encourage compliance with wartime policies. A student, however, may use the images of these broadsides as a means to portray the use of propaganda or embodiment of nationalism. This use of the works is clearly transformative in that their use in the video varies greatly from their original purpose. Transformation can also be achieved through the use of copyrighted materials for commentary or parody. The good news for teachers considering a documentary project is that much of the way students use material in a film does indeed transform the nature of the works.

What exactly is copyrighted? Students may assume that only resources with the copyright notice (©) are actually copyrighted. This is not accurate. In fact, anything that has been fixed in a tangible medium (e.g., image file, printed or distributed text, music files) is copyrighted whether it is marked as such or not. In fact, when students export their films to a movie file, their work is copyrighted. The copyright notice indicates that the copyright is registered with the U.S. Copyright Office. So whether or not a notice is provided, students (and teachers) should consider any work or resources they find in books and online as protected by copyright.

Creative Commons as a Copyright Alternative

While copyright law and fair use have been in place since 1976, a new effort to put the control of rights directly into the hands of the creator has recently been developed—Creative Commons licensing—developed in 2001 by a nonprofit group to enable creators to specify which specific rights they wish to retain and those that they relinquish. While Creative Commons licensing doesn't replace copyright, it eliminates the need for negotiations between the licensor and licensee to make the process of using copyrighted works within parameters designated by the licensor.

There are four standard Creative Commons licenses from which creators can choose:

- Attribution: Licensees may copy, distribute, display, and perform the work and make derivative works based on it only if they give the author or licensor the credits in the manner specified by these.
- Share-alike: Licensees may distribute derivative works only under a license identical to the license that governs the original work.
- Noncommercial: Licensees may copy, distribute, display, and perform the work and make derivative works based on it only for noncommercial purposes.
- No derivative works: Licensees may copy, distribute, display, and perform only verbatim copies of the work, not derivative works based on it.

Creators can choose the parameters for their license on the Creative Commons Web page: http://creativecommons.org/choose/. In discussing and deliberately choosing the type of license that students would like to govern their work, students may gain a new understanding and appreciation for the ethical use of materials created by others in their own work.

Follow Your School's Policies

While it may be interesting and enlightening to talk about different interpretations of copyright and fair use, ultimately you should follow your school's or division's policies and procedures related to copyright. If after reading this section and digging in to *Copyright Clarity* you think your school's policy is perhaps too restrictive, you may want to begin a discussion with administrators and school library media specialists about the recently released *Code of Best*

Practices in Fair Use for Media Literacy Education.[9] Adopted by the National Association for Media Literacy Education, the National Council of Teachers of English, and a number of other organizations, this Code of Best Practices provides excellent guidance to developing a more empowering approach to copyright in education. This document can serve as a catalyst for discussion and the reconsideration of copyright policies.

HOSTING, PUBLISHING, AND SHARING FILMS

As noted in the opening section of this chapter, there are many benefits of students sharing their work beyond the classroom. It is incredible to think about how video sharing sites literally create a worldwide audience. And the ability of viewers to comment on and rate student films is a powerful motivator and reinforcement for students. It's an incredible thing to see a student's face light up when he or she receives positive reactions to the work—perhaps from a teenager on the opposite side of the world!

Despite these benefits, however, sharing student work online also presents some challenges. First and foremost, school and school division policy may limit or prohibit sharing student work online. It is critical to carefully follow what is permitted and what is not. In some cases, sharing student work online is allowed only if protected by a password. In other cases, students may be able to post their work to a video sharing site only if commenting is disabled.

You may also be required to have student and parent release forms to post the work publicly. Many schools and divisions have blanket release forms that parents sign at the beginning of each year. While this technically may be enough consent to post students' work online, some parents may not be comfortable with making the work public in this way—particularly if their children are featured on camera. It is important to respect these concerns and allow students and parents to opt out as they wish.

If you are permitted to share your students' work online, there are a number of hosting services available. You'll want to consider each service's limitations and features. In some cases you can set privacy controls and/or passwords. With other hosting options, this may not be possible. To complicate matters further, some sites provide free hosting while others charge different tiers of fees, depending on the number and size of the movie files you upload. Table 7.1 will help you to explore a number of commonly used

Table 7.1. Online Video Hosting Options

Site	Cost	Per File Size/Total Storage Limit	Sharing Control	Sharing Type	Comments
YouTube	Free	2 GB/ None	Public/Private With Invitation	Link Embed Code Social Media	Yes
Vimeo	Free/Vimeo Plus $9.95 per month	Free: 500 MB per week/50 GB per year Plus: 5GB per week	Public/Private By Choice or Invitation	Link Embed Code Social Media	Yes
TeacherTube	Free	None/None	Public/Private With Invitation	Link Embed Code Social Media	No
SchoolTube	Free	2 GB/None	Public/Private With Invitation	Link Embed Code Social Media	No
Dropbox	Free/Pro $9.99 per month	Free: 2 GB/ 18 GB total Pro: 100, 200, or 500 GB	Private With Invitation	Link Shared via Email Address	No
Google Drive	Free/Can Purchase Additional Storage	5 GB	Public/Private With Invitation	Link Shared via Email Address	No

options for teachers and schools. It will be helpful, though, to consider your constraints before finding the most appropriate service.

Whatever service you choose, be sure to do your homework. Identify the file size limit for individual uploads and make sure that when students export their video files that they will fit within this constraint. Test out the process from uploading, to viewing the uploaded file, to the commenting and privacy options. The more you know about how the service works ahead of time, the smoother this process will be for you and your students. Once the films are uploaded, it's time to enjoy the show.

ROLLING OUT THE RED CARPET:
FILM FESTIVALS AND COMPETITIONS

When interviewed about how she prepared for a Hollywood film premiere, Diane Lane once said:

> I can tell you that, you know, when I went to my first movie premiere, it was my own movie, and I wore the best jeans I had and my favorite top. You know, I made sure my hair had some wave in it because I braided it the night before myself.[10]

These days, awards shows, festivals, and premieres have taken on a different status replete with red carpets, pre-event interviews, paparazzi, and swag. Often the event around a film can be as daunting (or impressive) as the making of a film itself! But you don't necessarily need to start shopping for red carpet by the yard or for a new gown or tuxedo to host a student film festival. In this section, you will explore a range of culminating experiences, from in-class film festivals to formal documentary competitions, and determine what type of event is best suited for you and your students. The important thing to remember is that the main purpose of any culminating experience is to give students an opportunity to share their work with others, celebrate the achievement, and discuss the films.

Film Festivals

Hosting or participating in a film festival for the classroom, school, or community is one way to share student-created documentaries. A film festival does not have to be too elaborate or onerous for the teacher. It could simply be a class period set aside to view student projects at the end of a production phase. You could pop some popcorn, hand out a program, and allow for some student conversation between films.

Most of the teachers featured in this book have veered in this direction. For example, Kelly, a fifth-grade teacher, invited the principal and collaborative teachers in to watch the films with the students. For parent/teacher conference day, she then set the films up on a laptop outside the classroom so that parents could watch the documentaries as they waited for their appointment with her. Eleventh-grade teacher Katie invited a jury panel including parents, professors, and administrators into the classroom to watch the student documentaries. After viewing the films, the panel gave juried awards to their favorite films.

To get into the spirit of a film festival, you will find some ideas below that might help get the juices flowing as you begin to envision what a film festival experience might look like in your classroom. A "must" is to print a program for viewers to both sequence the featured films and to provide a little ambiance for the festival. In figure 7.1a and 7.1b below, you see the cover of a

Figure 7.1a.

Mythbusters:
Setting the Record straight in American History
"It would be better not to know so many things than to know so many things that are not so." -- Felix Okoye

An Introduction to the Festival:

Over the past two to three weeks, students have been asked to create a "Ken Burns" documentary using Windows Movie Maker. The purpose of the documentary was to debunk, dispel or uphold a myth about a historical figure in American history. Students were given a number of "myth" choices (See Table below) along with an assembled archive of documents that could help them begin their research. Two students chose to develop their own myth and conduct independent research.

Myth #1	**Christopher Columbus** set out to prove the earth was round and died poor, penniless and unaware that he discovered a new continent.
Myth #2	**Pocahontas** fell for and saved John Smith as well as the settlers of the Jamestown colony.
Myth #3	**George Washington** chopped down the cherry tree and had wooden teeth.
Myth #4	**Betsey Ross** invented the American flag.
Myth #5	**Chief Seattle** gave a stirring speech in 1854 about preserving the environment.
Myth #6	**Rosa Parks** was tired and had no idea that she was about to do something important.
Myth #7	**Jackie Robinson** was the first black baseball player in the Major Leagues.
Myth #8	**Helen Keller's** historical significance lies in advocacy for the disabled.

Figure 7.1b.

program and the inside cover, which includes a description of the project and a list of the eight films by title.

These programs can become more elaborate if you choose to include a space for participants to take notes on each film or even a mini-rubric or feedback form for each documentary as a way to cue participants to think about particular elements of the films (table 7.2).

Table 7.2. Possible Rubric for Each Film in Film Festival

	Comments
Visual Effects (e.g., panning, zooming, transitions, text captions)	
Voice/Sound Communication (e.g., voice includes volume, diction, fluency, flow, inflection and sound includes music, effects, silence)	
Final Editing (e.g., timing of narration and images, pacing, titles and credits)	
Overall Impact of the Film	

You might even do a more simple feedback option that asks respondents to identify two to three elements of the film they enjoyed, one question they have related to the topic or production, and a friendly suggestion for future work.

Awards are another fun and rewarding aspect of hosting a film festival. The awards are intended to recognize the collective hard work that goes into the film projects and to provide a laugh or two, but not necessarily serve as a summative judgment about the final films. There are plenty of opportunities for assessment in the rubric covered in the previous four chapters. In table 7.3, we have listed some of the awards we have given in the past. As you can see, we like to have a little fun with our students. Please feel free to use these as your own or to create your own set of awards that best suits your students' sense of humor and/or your own instructional purpose.

Other film festival opportunities take students beyond the four walls of the classroom into experiences that are more elaborate in scope. In the recently published book *From Inspiration to Red Carpet: Hosting Your Own Film Festival*, Bass, Goodrich, and Lindskog chronicle their own experience of creating, managing, and hosting the Parkway Digital Film

Table 7.3. Sample Awards

Michael Moore's "I've got an ax to grind" award	Alexandra Pelosi's "Not afraid of a little controversy" award.
Daily Show's "I am going to be a Daily Show correspondent Edgy satire" award	Quentin Tarantino's "I'm-not-quite-sure-I-got- it-but-it-sure-is-hip" award.
Stanley Kubrick's "Off the wall—I think I'm trippin—avant-garde" award	Sophia Coppola's "Ain't I a Woman-Representin'" award
	Clint Eastwood's "Kickin' original score" award
Spike Lee's "Fight the Power'" award	
	Peter Jackson's "Most likely to have a sequel" award
Woody Allen's "I should get an award" award	
	Penny Marshall's "Most likely to be billed as a 'Chick flick'" award
Frank Capra's "I am oh so capraesque" award	
Coen brothers' "Collaboration" award	George Lucas' "Light Saber Special Effects" award
Oliver Stone's "Conspiracy" award	Cecil B. Demille's "Most likely to be on the Hallmark channel around the holidays" award
M. Night Shyamalan's "I didn't get it till the last six seconds" award	

Festival.[11] First held in 2008, the Parkway Film Festival is a district-wide culminating event for K–12 students wanting to showcase their digital projects. These projects are deeply rooted in social studies content and supported by the school's standards and curriculum, including direct ties to literacy with a clear focus on writing, reading, and digital literacy skills. While the festival is not focused entirely on documentary projects but also on digital storytelling, for the administrator, teacher, or instructional technologist wanting to make documentary making a centerpiece of a school's curriculum or culture, you should definitely check out the gold standard of the Parkway Digital Film Festival. On their website, they have many resources that might assist you in planning, including a film festival entry guide and a gallery of student film projects (http://www.pkwy.k12 .mo.us/tis/filmFestival/).

Film Competitions

Film competitions can also provide focus and motivation for a documentary film project. Highlighted below are two award-winning organizations offering students an opportunity to showcase their documentary work within national competitions.

National History Day

National History Day sponsors a yearlong academic program focused on historical research for elementary and secondary history students. In this award-winning contest, students choose historical topics related to a theme and conduct extensive primary and secondary research through libraries, archives, museums, oral history interviews, and historic sites. Upcoming themes for the competition include:

- 2014: Rights & Responsibilities in History
- 2015: Exploration, Encounter, Exchange in History
- 2016: Migration & Movement in History: People, Places, Ideas
- 2017: Taking a Stand in History

Students entering the competitions use the theme to guide a historical inquiry and then present their research in the form of original papers, Web sites, exhibits, performances, and documentaries. Students can enter these final projects into competitions at the local, state, and national level, where they are evaluated by professional historians and educators. On the National History Day Web site (http://www.nhd.org), the organization outlines the process, provides resources for teachers and students, and gives details about the competitions including information about scholarships and prizes for award-winning entries. For teachers wanting more information on creating a historical documentary, NHD has its own 56-page resource guide and DVD for sale on its Web site titled *How to Create a Historical Documentary*.[12] This easy-to-follow workbook and video gives step-by-step instructions for helping students develop documentaries.

C-Span StudentCam

StudentCam is C-SPAN's annual documentary competition encouraging students to think about issues that affect their communities and the nation. Students are asked to create a short (five- to eight-minute) video documentary on a topic related to the competition theme. In 2013, students created video on the theme *Message to the President: What's the most important issue that the president should consider in 2013?*

The competition is focused on secondary students with categories for middle and high school students. All documentaries must contain a small amount of supporting C-SPAN footage that relates to the chosen topic, and the students are encouraged to show various perspectives on any issue explored within the films. In 2013, C-SPAN gave 75 awards from the 1,300 entries—first prize receives $5,000, and the video is shown on C-SPAN.

On the StudentCam Web site (http://www.studentcam.org), there are how-to videos, rules for the competition, and an archive of the winning documentaries. Regardless of whether your students compete, you will find the videos a great resource for any classroom documentary project.

CONCLUSION

If you are overwhelmed with the prospect of a film premiere or competition, don't be. Remember to start slowly and simply give your students an opportunity to share their work. English actor Tom Felton once said, "You avoid the hype while you're working, you have to, but the premiere is the one night of the year where you can enjoy it." [13] However you choose to end the documentary experience, you and your students should enjoy it and know that you have crossed the threshold into the teaching elite, a category of "ambitious teachers." [14] In the next chapter, you will hear from fellow ambitious teachers who have also courageously tried a documentary project and lived to tell great stories and to give advice to those that dare to follow in their footsteps!

NOTES

1. "Roger Ebert: Film Critic and Blogger," TED.com, accessed August 22, 2013, http://www.ted.com/speakers/roger_ebert.html.

2. Matthew Kearney and Sandy Schuck, "Authentic Learning through the use of Video," (presentation, Australasian Computing Education Conference, Adelaide, Australia, July 2004); Stephen Ryan, "Digital Video: Using Technology to Improve Learner Motivation," *Modern English Teacher* 11, no. 2 (2002): 72–75.

3. Renee R. Hobbs, *Copyright Clarity: How Fair Use Supports Digital Learning* (Thousand Oaks, CA: Corwin, 2010).

4. Ibid., 17.

5. Ibid., 18.

6. United States Copyright Office, *Circular 92* (Washington, DC: Author, 2011).

7. Carrie Russell, *Complete Copyright* (Washington, DC: American Library Association, 2004): 19, as quoted in Hobbs, *Copyright Clarity*: 59.

8. Hobbs, *Copyright Clarity*: 18.

9. The Center for Social Media, *Code of Best Practices in Fair Use for Media Literacy Education*, 2013, http://www.centerforsocialmedia.org/fair-use/related-materials/codes/code-best-practices-fair-use-media-literacy-education

10. Joel Keller, "Diane Lane on Playing Pat Loud in 'Cinema Verite' . . . and Why She's Off the Pop Culture Grid," *Huffpost TV*, last modified April 22, 2011 (10:05 a.m.), http://www.aoltv.com/2011/04/22/diane-lane-cinema-verite-interview/

11. William L. Bass, Christian Goodrich, and Kim Lindskog, *From Inspiration to Red Carpet: Host Your Own Student Film Festival* (Washington, DC: International Society for Technology in Education, 2013).

12. National History Day, *How to Create a Historical Documentary: A Guide to Creating Historical Documentaries* (College Park, MD: NHD, 2008), http://www.nhd.org/cart/index.php?main_page=product_info&products_id=3

13. "Tom Felton," *BrainyQuotes*, accessed August 22, 2013, http://www.brainyquote.com/quotes/quotes/t/tomfelton472969.html.

14. S. G. Grant and Jill Gradwell, eds., *Teaching History with Big Ideas: Cases of Ambitious Teaching* (Lanham, MD: Rowman & Littlefield, 2010).

8

IT'S A WRAP

Parting Thoughts to Executive Producers

Filmmaking is a completely imperfect art form that takes years and, over those years, the movie tells you what it is. Mistakes happen, accidents happen and true great films are the results of those mistakes and the decisions that those directors make during those moments.

—Jason Reitman[1]

Throughout this book you have had an opportunity to peer into a number of classrooms through the examples embedded in the chapters. In this chapter, some of these teachers will speak directly to you about their experience, the lessons they've learned, and the advice they offer. The stories they share are honest impressions of the documentary-making experience. As with any complex classroom experience, there are simply things you wish you had known to smooth out the kinks or to anticipate the trouble spots. We asked the teachers to focus on these areas by responding to the following prompt: *If I had only known then what I know now about the documentary film process, I would have . . .*

It is important to note that the teachers featured in this chapter are first and foremost classroom teachers, but they are looking for ways to use technology in meaningful ways. They see documentary making as a way of connecting to the academic discipline they teach but rooted in 21st-century literacy experiences that their students crave. They also see this instructional opportunity as worthwhile but a complex undertaking. Thus, they offer a range of perspectives—from those teachers that focus on tricks of the trade when it comes to technology (e.g., the use of Dropbox to manage files) to those that struggle with guiding students in the creative aspects of documentary projects (e.g., should you limit music selections?).

These teachers are like you—they are *ambitious*. Grant and Gradwell describe ambitious teachers as those teachers who "deeply understand their subject matter and they actively seek ways to connect that subject matter with the lived experiences of their students. They often do so, however, while facing contextual factors . . . that may push them in different directions."[2] To design and implement a digital documentary project in the standards-based, assessment-oriented environment today is clearly an ambitious endeavor. The purpose of this chapter is to connect you with colleagues who have been there and to offer parting thoughts before you tackle your own classroom documentary experience.

KIM TABLER, MARYVILLE ELEMENTARY, KENTUCKY

If I had only known then what I know now about the documentary film process, I would have done a few things differently. To begin, I would make documentaries after students have some background for the topic, not as the introduction to a topic or subject. My first documentary project was done with elementary students who had limited social studies exposure due to time and the curriculum map from younger grades. Topic discovery is great, but they need some background knowledge to be able to make relevant connections to the material. By having some understanding of the topic, students are able to write their scripts into a narrative that is punctuated by evidence. In this first experience, students inserted evidence back-to-back and nearly word for word from the documents—not necessarily plagiarism because they did change the wording—but the narratives weren't written in language students their age and younger would understand. We had to do a lot of editing to encourage students to find their voice and to not rely too heavily on the documents for the narrative.

I would also do some modeling and direct lessons on evaluating primary sources to use in the documentaries. Even if you select an archive of images and documents ahead of time, students need experience with evaluating sources and using evidence as well as using evidence within a script. When we first started this project, I just had students pick out what they thought went well with their section, but after seeing what they selected we had to have some conversations about the choices they make around soundtrack, image selection, and text. When I would talk to them about why they chose certain images or documents, often their selections did not reflect their intention. We then had to evaluate if what they chose was truly the best, or if one of the other images or documents would have been better. If they had had the previous lessons on evaluating these sources, we may not have had to have as much editing time on this part of the project. As it was, students just picked what they thought looked nice, not necessarily what matched the narrative they were constructing.

Lastly, I would have developed a library of sources and sites that students could use as they were making their documentaries. Having sites and sources readily available for students to find their primary sources would speed up the research process. Without this classroom archive, the research part of the project almost took double the time. It does require a little more planning, but in the long run it makes for better projects and less frustration.

KATIE BOOTH, SCOTT COUNTY HIGH SCHOOL, KENTUCKY

If I had only known then what I know now about the documentary film process, I would have provided formative checkpoints and products throughout the documentary process. As an advanced placement teacher, it was so easy to dive right into the work, trusting this highly motivated group to work with freedom, flexibility, and the independence to forge ahead in their excitement over the final product. In retrospect, that is a mistake!

I chose to do one large digital documentary with my class of AP world history students as a summative product for our yearlong course. We broke the film up into segments, with small groups of students taking responsibility for each part of the whole film. This class of students was, as might be expected, highly capable and motivated. In releasing them to do this work, I relied on their maturity and strong academic abilities to carry the project forward without considering how having a group of 30 students all working in smaller, interdependent groups might impact our ability to come together with a cohesive project.

At the beginning of the project, we held whole-class planning meetings to settle on our central research question. When this was done, the research portion began, which consisted of a series of individual workdays driven by large, guiding questions I constructed for the students to answer. Looking back, it would have been helpful to establish biweekly meetings for everyone to check in so that we wouldn't have experienced overlap or disjointedness as we continued.

By about the end of the second week of the project, I could feel the individual component parts beginning to spiral away from one another, so I began to attempt to pull the threads back together. Students had to come together with their ideas for each portion of the project in a documentary proposal meeting. Each group presented their segment of the documentary to adults who were either present in the classroom or video conferenced in for the occasion. This meeting helped lend a serious tone to the work we were doing, as well as gave students an opportunity to articulate their thinking and work as a team moving toward the same vision of the class film project.

After this initial hiccup, we began to hold more regular meetings, usually briefly before the day's work began. Looking back, I would go further and be much more specific in terms of deadlines. These kinds of periodic checkpoints would help to ensure that each group worked out kinks in their scripts and picture choice, as well as in terms of inputting that information into Movie Maker. At the time, I was very concerned about stifling their creativity and didn't want my facilitation to put a damper on their work—making them feel like I was looking over their shoulder to hinder their ability to feel free in the creative process. However, the product lends itself so much to creativity; imposing deadlines for specific components would not have impacted them as much as I thought.

JAMES WALSH, SCOTT COUNTY HIGH SCHOOL, KENTUCKY (FORMERLY AT LEXINGTON TRADITIONAL MAGNET MIDDLE SCHOOL)

If I had only known then what I know now about the documentary film process, I would have made sure my students received "compensatory damages" from my initial attempts. I tried documentary making my first year teaching, and so I experienced a pretty steep learning curve. My students surely deserved something for their work as subjects in my documentary experiment. Despite the success I experienced with my first foray into doing digital documentaries, there are at least three things I would change in future attempts—preparation, modeling, and creative direction.

As with any project-based assessment, success comes from adequate preparation. This applies especially to digital documentaries. I wish I would have begun the process by making a documentary myself, but not on the subject matter the students will tackle. A strong model would have given students a clearer idea of the end product and would have helped to avoid an elaborate slide presentation on the part of the students. Also, I would have saved time in the computer lab by providing students with a database of possible images—this would have also helped students select strong and supporting imagery for their film. Online collections of materials such as Digital Docs in a Box are perfect starting places for streamlining the documentary process.

One of my weaknesses in my short tenure as a teacher has been modeling lessons and transitions effectively. Modeling and transitions are essential to this project. In addition to creating my own digital documentary, at each stage of the process, I plan to demonstrate to the class how to do each step, whether by document camera or simply walking the room. It sounds basic, but it's something I need to remind myself of daily.

I would also provide more time for the pre-production phases and less for the computer time to actually complete the videos. The more time students spend in the research, pre-writing, storyboarding, and scriptwriting, the more successful and efficient the production phase will be. I would have felt more comfortable in providing latitude and freedom on the "creative" aspects of the production if I was more confident that the research and content had been covered adequately.

These "next time" steps will hopefully provide my students with a more efficient and effective experience to what was an already excellent project. Like anything worth doing in inquiry-based social studies learning, this experience requires work—both preparatory and daily during the process.

JASON HOWARD, WOODFORD COUNTY HIGH SCHOOL, KENTUCKY

If I had only known then what I know now about the documentary film process, I would have eased students into the process and more efficiently managed the technical aspects of the documentary projects. The first time I tried documentary work in my classroom, it went well—all things considered—but there are definitely a lot of practical steps that needed to be taken to make it a smooth process beginning to end on future attempts.

The first thing I would do is set up a class Dropbox (http://dropbox. com). In a Dropbox, students (i.e., groups) can be assigned folders that only group members can access. This solves a lot of issues with "student X is missing today and he/she had all our research." While that can (and does) still happen even after instituting a Dropbox, the groups were not held back as much, as the materials can be housed online and the students can manage it—and they can access their files if they wish to work on things at home. The Dropbox also makes formative checks much easier, as I can check on the progress made by the groups from anywhere, at any time.

I would have also asked students to turn in their final films via a YouTube account. The first time I tried documentary work, I had students turning in their documentaries on burned DVDs, flash drives, or e-mail. Managing the files in all of these forms was a nightmare and required extra work in reorganizing the films into one location for a class screening. While you could also use Dropbox for this, I prefer YouTube because it is set up and ready to go for the "big premiere" at the end of the unit.

I would have also eased students into the documentary process by starting the students out with short, minute-long productions that could be made in a class period or two. Once they mastered some of the filmmaking basics, then we could move toward a more elaborated filmmaking experience. As I have gained more experience with student-created documentaries, I have created checkpoints that guide students through the research, storyboard, and image collection processes. It will be interesting to see how this works when I have an entire school year to work students through the process.

DAVID CARPENTER, WASHINGTON INTERNATIONAL SCHOOL, WASHINGTON, D.C.

If I had only known then what I know now about the documentary film process, I would have given students more opportunities to analyze good and poorly de-

signed presentations as a way to build their foundation knowledge of design. It is valuable to immerse the students in a variety of documentary film projects to help them develop a critical eye for film. Teachers can use classroom discussion to help the students better understand the structure, strengths, and weaknesses of the videos they watched. To further these analytic skills, I try to make sure the students always have the project rubric in hand as they prepare and shoot their video. My rubrics list assessment criteria but also contain questions to get the students to think about their audience, their intent, and how they are introducing and building characters, as well as additional technical criteria.

Logistics and adult supervision come into play, especially with elementary and middle school students. It may be helpful to work with the students to write up a code of conduct for when they are out in the school shooting their scenes. It is helpful to work with administration to get their take on how much freedom students can have in filming in the cafeteria, classrooms, etc., when an adult might not always be present. Finding spaces to record videos in one's school is not an easy task. Even if a space is open, students and adults walking through the area can be a problem. Background noise, especially in hallways, is another obstacle that the student videographers must problem solve around.

SEAN MORAN, THE DIRECTOR OF TECHNOLOGY FOR WASHINGTON INTERNATIONAL SCHOOL

If I had only known then what I know now about the documentary film process, I would not *have assumed the exposure to volumes of digital video (films, television, Internet memes) prepared students to be creators of film.* I learned that the reality is just the opposite. The majority of digital video viewed by the average adolescent succeeds in capturing attention in spite of poor production values, a lack of understanding of film grammar, and a complete disregard for story structure. Because of this, students never learn a vocabulary of composition or structure that can help them create their own documentaries.

First and foremost, it's all about the story. Without story, a documentary is just a collection of facts. To this end, the script is key. Starting with a well-researched premise and continuing through diligently transcribed interviews, making sure the building blocks of the script are solid, will position any student filmmaker in creating a documentary that resonates with its audience. This is incredibly detailed work and requires patience—even before students actually create the documentary.

Research, treatments, scripts, and storyboards—these are the things that separate real documentaries from funny cat videos on YouTube. The shooting of B-roll and the editing of the film should almost be mechanical tasks in realizing the vision of the film. So often with students, the planning happens after they've checked out the equipment and are about to shoot. Aside from being inefficient, it also never leads to good decision making.

Teaching students basic film vocabulary is key to successful documentary projects. Just a simple explanation of the types of shots (long shot, medium shot, close-up), basic editing principles (edit on an angle or an action, or cut to a different size), and camera and lighting techniques (avoiding zooms, maintaining headroom and eyeline, three-point lighting) will help students pull everything together. A student can have detailed documentation for locations and shots and interview questions, but unless that student understands the aesthetic tradition in a really basic way, the final film will look like a home video.

Deconstructing good documentary films is the best way to model good technique. From analyzing specific shots and editing choices to looking at narrative arc and depictions of specific characters, pulling apart good films is essential before allowing students to pick up cameras.

At the end of the day, student films can be wildly successful projects without looking particularly polished. Student internalization of the lessons of the production process (planning, teamwork, the manipulation of the film's message to communicate an idea to an audience) is the ultimate goal. Generally, good product follows good process, but "good product" is a squishier concept and, especially in the hands of a novice filmmaker, can be more elusive.

LAUREN GALLICCHIO, BRYAN STATION HIGH SCHOOL, KENTUCKY

If I had only known then what I know now about the documentary film process, I would have been prepared to be the technical expert in the room. When

I first began to implement the documentary film work into my curriculum, I was aware of some of the pitfalls and challenges of this type of project: scheduling the necessary computer lab time, scaffolding for heterogeneous student groups, keeping the digital materials organized, etc.

After several project iterations, I became an expert at navigating my school's computer lab but secretly hoped that as students learned the moviemaking platform, my role as technical expert could shift to the students. At some point, I thought my students would bridge the generational gap and surpass my knowledge of technology. Surprisingly, I am still the most technically "fluent" person in the classroom. I realized that even though students' exposure and use of technology has increased dramatically, they use it very superficially. Yes, they can text. Yes, they can use the Internet on their smartphone. Yes, they can update their Facebook status. But, rarely does a student know how to use technology to create a multimedia project to demonstrate understanding of a concept or idea. As a result, I haven't been able to relinquish my role as technical adviser in the documentary process.

For example, I have learned about the importance of digital file formats and issues of compatibility within the moviemaking program. For example, if a student is creating a movie using Microsoft Movie Maker, he or she cannot use a song from his or her iTunes library without first converting it to an MP3 file. This seems easy enough, but issues of file compatibility compound when 30 students are simultaneously learning the same lesson. Since students don't usually create their own multimedia projects, they can sometimes forget that not all pieces of technology are compatible. I have found working with a "digital media bank"—a selection of images and songs that will be compatible with the video editing program—has been a helpful tool in overcoming one of the technical glitches that can sometimes derail the precious time in the computer lab.

Teaching students about communicating ideas through the documentary medium has also been tricky. For example, I have enjoyed coaching students as they explore the creative aspects of documentaries. This is a wonderful opportunity for the student but can lead to some difficulties for the teacher during the assessment process if students do not focus on connecting the video elements with the narrative of the film. If students do not understand how a song can support an idea or how an image can really emphasize a statement, then the students will more than likely select a song or an image simply because they like it. Part of my job is to nudge students to think about the aesthetic choices they make and the way in which they support their interpretation.

JOSEPH KARB, 7TH AND 8TH GRADE SOCIAL STUDIES TEACHER, SPRINGVILLE-GRIFFITH MIDDLE SCHOOL

BENJAMIN HIGGINS, TECHNOLOGY INTEGRATION SPECIALIST, SPRINGVILLE-GRIFFITH CENTRAL SCHOOL DISTRICT

If we had only known what we know now about the documentary film process, we would have required students to complete their research and planning before they began using video editing software. During our initial attempt at student documentary making, we allowed students to begin producing their documentary video while they were researching topics and planning their documentary. We did provide some general suggestions regarding logical steps in the video creation process, but each group was allowed to decide how best to proceed to complete their documentary.

Of course, most middle and high school students, if given the choice, will choose the more interactive option first. So instead of carefully researching and planning their projects, the majority of students completed basic research and then immediately started using the video editing software to "play" with transitions, graphics, and sound effects. Others started looking for the perfect song to use as background music or the perfect photos to illustrate their topic. Once they became involved with this multimedia binge, it became very difficult to redirect students back to complete the necessary research, planning, and writing necessary for an effective documentary. Without a solid foundation of research, our students' efforts paid few dividends in the end because most of their documentaries were lacking in substance and scattered.

When we complete documentaries with our students today, we require them to follow a relatively prescribed procedure that includes framing a question, researching, creating a story board, finding photographs and video clips, writing a script, and then using the video editing software to create their documentaries (finding the perfect song comes last). After each step, students are required to show us their work and get our approval before they go on to the next step in the process. Highlighting model examples of past work has also been a great way to reinforce the necessary elements of film making without having to spend time teaching cinematography. Using this procedure has dramatically improved the quality of our student documentaries.

Documentary making is hard work for both students and teachers. Students have to research, find images, record video, write a script, edit their work, with the end goal of creating a compelling video that tells a story. But with the proper guidance, video making is incredibly rewarding work that can be a fantastic learning experience.

PARTING THOUGHTS

No one ever said teaching was easy—rewarding, sure—but not easy. Filmmaking in the classroom is no different. The documentary process is messy even for the professionals. Even with the detailed supports, phases, and assessment opportunities provided in this book, you will learn on the job. As you evolve the documentary experience in your own context with your own students, you will always find things that you could streamline, improve, and customize the next time you take on the challenge. It's critical to give yourself the space and permission to make mistakes and learn from them. The same could be said for your students. It takes an ambitious teacher to take on (and pull off) a classroom documentary project. You're just that teacher. We hope that you've found a helpful starting place in this book—a launch point for you to begin your journey in documentary making. So, quiet on the set. Places everyone! Aaaaaaannnnnnnd action!

NOTES

1. Radheyan Simonpillai, "Jason Reitman Interview," *AskMen*, http://www.ask men.com/celebs/interview_300/369_jason-reitman-interview.html.
2. S. G. Grant and Jill Gradwell, eds., *Teaching History with Big Ideas: Cases of Ambitious Teaching* (Lanham, MD: Rowman & Littlefield, 2010): vii.

APPENDIX A

Four-Phase Documentary Rubric

Table A1.1. Research Phase

	Developing Basic Skills	Approaching Standard	At Standard	Exceeds Standard
Building background knowledge	Guiding question(s) were answered partially and/or with minor inaccuracies.	Guiding question(s) were answered or with minor inaccuracies.	Guiding question(s) were answered accurately and completely.	Guiding question(s) were answered accurately and completely in a comprehensive and nuanced way.
Developing an argument	Argument lacks focus or clarity.	Argument is focused and clear.	Argument is focused, clear and supported with evidence.	Argument is focused, clear, insightful and supported with multiple sources of evidence.
Using evidence	Answers to research question(s) were not supported with evidence (e.g., data, images, quotations, etc.).	Answers to research question(s) were supported with only a few sources of evidence (e.g., data, images, quotations, etc.).	Answers to research question(s) were supported with a variety of evidence (e.g., data, images, quotations, etc.).	Answers to research question(s) were supported with a variety of evidence (e.g., data, images, quotations, etc.) representing multiple perspectives.

Table A1.2. Documentary Treatment Phase

	Developing Basic Skills	Approaching Standard	At Standard	Exceeds Standard
Theme	The theme of the film is not clearly articulated.	The theme of the film is either not clearly articulated or does not fit well with the approach to the topic.	The theme of the film is clearly articulated and fits with the approach to the topic.	The theme of the film is clearly articulated and provides a compelling lens through which to approach the topic.
Structure	The structure is either not stated or does not fit well with the argument or theme.	The structure selected for the film might work, but another approach would be preferable.	The structure selected for the film is appropriate, given their argument and theme.	The structure selected is ideally suited for the focus of the film.
Pitch	The pitch either lacks clarity and/or provides only a limited sense of the purpose of the film.	The pitch is mostly clear and provides a sense of the purpose for the film, including the guiding question.	The pitch is clear and provides a detailed overview of the purpose for the film, including the guiding question.	The pitch is clear and provides a compelling purpose for the film.
Outlining the narrative	The outline of the film is unclear and/or not coherent.	The outline of the film lacks some detail and/or coherence.	The outline of the film is clear and coherent.	The outline of the film is clear and well-organized, creating a sense of rising action throughout.
Using evidence	The outline of the film includes minimal use of data, quotations, etc. from sources.	The outline of the film includes data, quotations, etc. from sources, but does not necessarily elaborate the narrative.	The outline of the film includes data, quotations, etc. from sources to elaborate the narrative.	The outline of the film describes a cogent use of data, quotations, etc. from sources to elaborate the narrative.

Table A1.3. Storyboard Phase

	Developing Basic Skills	Approaching Standard	At Standard	Exceeds Standard
Selecting imagery	Images selected are not high quality, not relevant, or varied.	Images selected are of high quality (i.e., not grainy or too much text), mostly relevant and are somewhat varied (e.g., people, places, objects).	Images selected are of high quality (i.e. not grainy or too much text), mostly relevant and are somewhat varied (e.g., people, places, objects).	Images selected are of high quality (i.e., not grainy or too much text), relevant and varied (e.g., people, places, objects).
Connecting imagery	Use of images and visual effects are not well connected with the narrative of the script.	Use of images and visual effects are mostly connected with the narrative of the script.	Use of images and visual effects connect with the narrative of the script.	Use of images and visual effects connect with the narrative and enrich the script.
Developing the script	Script is structured and organized according to the treatment but not developed.	Script is structured and organized according to the treatment and partially developed.	Script is structured and organized according to the treatment and adequately developed.	Script is structured and organized according to the treatment and fully developed with appropriate detail, evidence, and transitions.
Enhancing the narrative	Narrative does not use techniques (dialogue, description, use of first person) effectively.	Narrative uses techniques (dialogue, description, use of first person) ineffectively.	Script effectively uses at least one technique (dialogue, description, use of first person) to develop experiences, events, and/or characters.	Script effectively uses a variety of techniques (dialogue, description, use of first person) to develop experiences, events, and/ or characters.

Table A1.4. Film Production Phase

	Developing Basic Skills	Approaching Standard	At Standard	Exceeds Standard
Using Visual Effects	Use of images and visual effects (e.g., panning, zooming, transitions, text captions) is not well connected with the narrative of the film.	Use of images and visual effects (e.g., panning, zooming, transitions, text captions) is mostly connected with the narrative of the film.	Use of visual effects (e.g., panning, zooming, transitions, text captions) is well-connected with the narrative of the film.	Use of images and visual effects (e.g., panning, zooming, transitions, text captions) enhances/enriches the film.
Voice/Sound Communication	Narration (volume, diction, fluency, flow, inflection) and use of audio (music, effects, silence) are not well connected to the tone, style, and theme of the film.	Narration (volume, diction, fluency, flow, inflection) and use of audio (music, effects, silence) connects with the tone, style, and theme of the film.	Narration (volume, diction, fluency, flow, inflection) and use of audio (music, effects, silence) contributes to the tone, style, and theme of the film.	Narration (volume, diction, fluency, flow, inflection) and use of audio (music, effects, silence) are integral in telling the story.
Final Editing	The final editing of the film (timing of narration and images, pacing, titles and credits) is not acceptable and/or detracts from the story.	The final editing of the film (timing of narration and images, pacing, titles and credits) is acceptable and does not detract from the story.	The final editing of the film (timing of narration and images, pacing, titles and credits) is mostly polished.	The final editing of the film (timing of narration and images, pacing, titles and credits) is polished and enhances story.
Overall Impact of the Film	The overall impact of the film is limited. The film does not adequately portray the interpretation of the film.	The overall impact of the film is mostly positive. The film adequately portrays the interpretation of the film.	The overall impact of the film is positive. The film effectively portrays the interpretation of the film.	The overall impact of the film is powerful. The film effectively portrays the interpretation of the film.

APPENDIX B

Blank Core Argument Template

I/We argue that _____

_____

because:

    Claim 1 _____

_____

      Supporting Evidence A:

      Supporting Evidence B:

      Supporting Evidence C:

    Claim 2 _____

_____

      Supporting Evidence A:

      Supporting Evidence B:

      Supporting Evidence C:

    Claim 3 _____

_____

      Supporting Evidence A:

      Supporting Evidence B:

      Supporting Evidence C:

APPENDIX C

Sample Core Argument

We argue that throughout the Great Depression, migrants' struggle to find a sense of place led many to suffer from a lack of identity because:

1. Economic hardship created professional and geographic displacement.
   a. "Drought in the Great Plains: A Case Study of Research on Climate and Society in the USA," by R. A. Warrick, in *Climatic Constraints and Human Activities* (1980)
      - In the 1930s, drought covered the entire plains for almost a decade. The drought's direct effect is most often remembered as agricultural. Many crops were damaged by deficient rainfall, high temperatures, and high winds, as well as insect infestations and dust storms that accompanied these conditions. The resulting agricultural depression contributed to the Great Depression's bank closures, business losses, increased unemployment, and other physical and emotional hardships. Although records focus on other problems, the lack of precipitation would also have affected wildlife and plant life, and would have created water shortages for domestic needs.
   b. *Farming the Dust Bowl: A First-Hand Account from Kansas*, by Lawrence Svobida (1986)
      - Firsthand account of a farmer trying and finally giving up and moving west.

2. Thousands of midwestern farmers were forced into a nomadic life-style.
   a. *American Exodus: The Dust Bowl Migration and Okie Culture in California*, by James Gregory (1989)
      * The Okies who went to the San Joaquin Valley went there primarily because farm work was familiar to them (53).
      * To lure them, California farmers had originally sent out flyers because the professionalized agriculture of California needed workers; they were seen as a "reliable pool of temporary workers who could move about the state with the rhythms of the growing season" (56).
      * Except for cotton, potatoes, and peas, Okies were not hired for fieldwork, which was relegated to nonwhites only (56).
      * They did "ladder-work" (fruit picking), an occupation with which they had very limited experience (56).
   b. "Why We Come To California"—FSA interview with Ms. Flora Robertson (1940)
      * Audio recording found online through the Library of Congress (http://www.loc.gov/item/afcts.4120b1)
      * Describes the challenges of traveling to California and her attitude about having to leave
   c. "Interview about life in Oklahoma and how and why he came to California (part 1 of 2)"—FSA interview with Tom Higginbotham (1940)
      * Audio recording found online through Library of Congress (http://www.loc.gov/item/afcts.4149a1)
      * Describes how he was unable to provide for family in Oklahoma so he came to California for work.
   d. "Depression Farming: Drought, Dust and Displacement," by T. H. Watkins, in *The 1930s* (2000)
      * Okies provided a big pool and soon numbered nearly half the state's migrant farm workers (93).
3. Limited opportunities and judgment by others re-emphasized their nomadic existence.
   a. *Children of the Dust Bowl: The True Story of the School at Weed-patch Camp*, by Jerry Stanley (1992)

- The culture was then proliferated through the social and economic separation in which the Okies lived. Okies associated only with Okies. Socially this isolation was caused by Okies banding together in tightly knit social groups for support in their new and often unfriendly home (35). They were not welcome anywhere outside their own communities. A plethora of signs posted on stores declared "Okies-Go Home!" (34).
- Although the rural Okies who migrated to California's farms in the 1930s came with nothing and when they arrived found almost less than nothing, they persisted, enduring countless hardships, and finally carving a niche for themselves and for their newly developed culture in the fields of California.
- Beth Stewart remembered her husband, Cory, got into a fight when he went to find a job at a cannery. Cory saw a sign at the cannery office that read NO JOBS FOR OKIES. (38)
- The children had been out of school so long they could not read or write. Teachers would ignore them. (38)

b. "Migrant agricultural worker's family. Seven hungry children. Mother aged thirty-two. Father is native Californian. Nipomo, California"—photograph by Dorothea Lange (1936)

- Found online through Library of Congress (http://www.loc. gov/pictures/resource/ppmsca.03054/)
- Shows family living in poor conditions; makeshift house shows how they are always on the move

APPENDIX D

Blank Documentary Treatment Template

STEP 1—THE PITCH

This film is about _____.
The film will be structured as a(n) (please circle one)
- character-driven
- event-driven
- issue-driven

narrative so that _____.
The question we want to explore is _____.

STEP 2—NARRATIVE OUTLINE

Act One—The Introduction

- How will you introduce your main character, topic, or issue? When will you begin your story?
    a. For a character-driven film, will you begin at the end of a person's life? At the beginning? In the midst of a crisis?
    b. For an issue-driven film, will you build toward a problem? Introduce the problem and then backtrack in the following acts toward context and cause?

   c. For an event-driven film, will you begin within the event? Start in quieter times and build toward crisis?

- How will you introduce your question that you will explore in the film to the viewers?

Act Two—The Body

- What three to four points do you want to make in the body of the film that will help to answer the question you pose in the introduction?
- How would you sequence these (chronologically, building action, etc.) in a way that helps your viewers explore the question?
- How can you represent these points by using various kinds of evidence you've collected?
- How will you set up the resolution, or "answer," to your question?

Act Three—The Conclusion

- What thoughts do you want to leave your viewers with?
- Will you summarize your question and evidence? If so, how will you do this?
- What questions do you want to linger in the minds of the viewers?
- How will you bring resolution to your film (doesn't mean end—means closure) for the viewers?

APPENDIX E

Sample Documentary Treatment

STEP 1—THE PITCH

This film is about the <u>challenges and lost sense of place that displaced farmers experienced during the Dust Bowl</u>.

The film will be structured as a(n) (please check one)

- character-driven
- event-driven
- issue-driven

narrative so that <u>it presents the large-scale impact of the Dust Bowl. It affected millions of people</u>.

The question we want to explore is <u>How does humanity respond when their livelihood is challenged?</u>

STEP 2—NARRATIVE OUTLINE

Act One—The Introduction

- How will you introduce your main character, topic, or issue? When will you begin your story?
  <u>We will introduce the issue by talking about the natural movement of mankind—we have always moved. However, what happens when the movement is not caused by a desire to see what lies beyond but is</u>

instead caused by an event so horrific that you have no choice? Enter the Dust Bowl.

a. For a character-driven film, will you begin at the end of a person's life? At the beginning? In the midst of a crisis?

b. For an issue-driven film, will you build toward a problem? Introduce the problem and then backtrack in the following acts toward context and cause?

While there will be a brief moment in the introduction that does not jump right into the Dust Bowl, we will dive right into the event to get viewers' attention right off the bat. Even though the focus of the documentary is not entirely the Dust Bowl itself but rather the social fallout that resulted from it, the Dust Bowl is the "star" of the film, and it is the central piece of history being discussed. However, the documentary will look at the toll it had on society rather than focus on the particulars of the event itself.

c. For an event-driven film, will you begin within the event? Start in quieter times and build toward crisis?

- How will you introduce your question that you will explore in the film to the viewers?

After providing some background information about the Dust Bowl, we will pose a question that gets to the heart of the film—what do you do?

Act Two—The Body

- What three to four points do you want to make in the body of the film that will help to answer the question you pose in the introduction?

1. Economic hardship created professional and geographic displacement.

2. Thousands of midwestern farmers were forced into a nomadic lifestyle.

3. Limited opportunities and judgment by others re-emphasized their nomadic existence.

- How would you sequence these (chronologically, building action, etc.) in a way that helps your viewers explore the question?

They will be sequenced as ordered above. The Dust Bowl is a catalyst for these changes, and they build in this way—like throwing a pebble (the

Dust Bowl) and watching the ripples. The initial ripple is the devastation that resulted in economic hardship. Next, the film will move to people like Lawrence Svobioda who gave up and moved west—thousands, perhaps millions, of people moved away from the Dust Bowl-stricken areas. Lastly, after all of this movement the question: What happened to all of these people that moved? Sadly, there is no real happy ending here for the generation struck by the Dust Bowl. Their children and grandchildren would be the ones that eventually would be accepted into society.

- How can you represent these points by using various kinds of evidence you've collected?
  The evidence comes from the U.S. government, interviews, and personal journals. It includes photographs, statistics, interviews, and political cartoons. It is important to bring in different perspectives, and we try to do that by drawing from several sources.

- How will you set up the resolution, or "answer," to your question?
  After laying out the evidence we will transition to what few rays of sunshine there were for Dust Bowl refugees—Woody Guthrie and FDR's policies. But ultimately, it is a story of too little, too late. The damage had been done, and it would be felt for generations. The resolution to the film is simply the resolve the Dust Bowl refugees showed in clinging to their identities even in the face of all of this hardship.

Act Three—The Conclusion

- What thoughts do you want to leave your viewers with?
  We want viewers to walk away wondering how they would respond in such a situation—both as the forced migrant and as a member of a community to which people migrate. Hopefully, by seeing the plight—the total devastation—viewers will see the Dust Bowl as a real event whose devastation was felt for generations.

- Will you summarize your question and evidence? If so, how will you do this?
  We won't summarize all the evidence but will emphasize persistence in the face of challenge. Hopefully the film will come full circle at the end and make it clear there really was no happy ending for that first generation of Dust Bowl migrants.

- What questions do you want to linger in the minds of the viewers?

  The film does not address the United States' emergence from the Great Depression, so hopefully viewers are encouraged to investigate what ultimately happened to the Dust Bowl refugees and their families. Viewers might also be led to think about any comparisons to current events, like Hurricane Katrina, Super Storm Sandy, or the Japanese tsunami. Did these events impact human movement and identity in similar ways?

- How will you bring resolution to your film (doesn't mean end—means closure) for the viewers?

  The final image in the film will be the "Migrant Mother" from the Dorothea Lange collection, which captures all of the emotion of the Dust Bowl. It shows the worries, the fear, the uncertainty, and even a glimpse of hope. It had to be a nightmare to live through it all, but people fought and clung to survive and recapture the life they once knew. It is a remarkable story and is written entirely on the migrant mother's facial expression.

APPENDIX F
Blank Storyboard Template

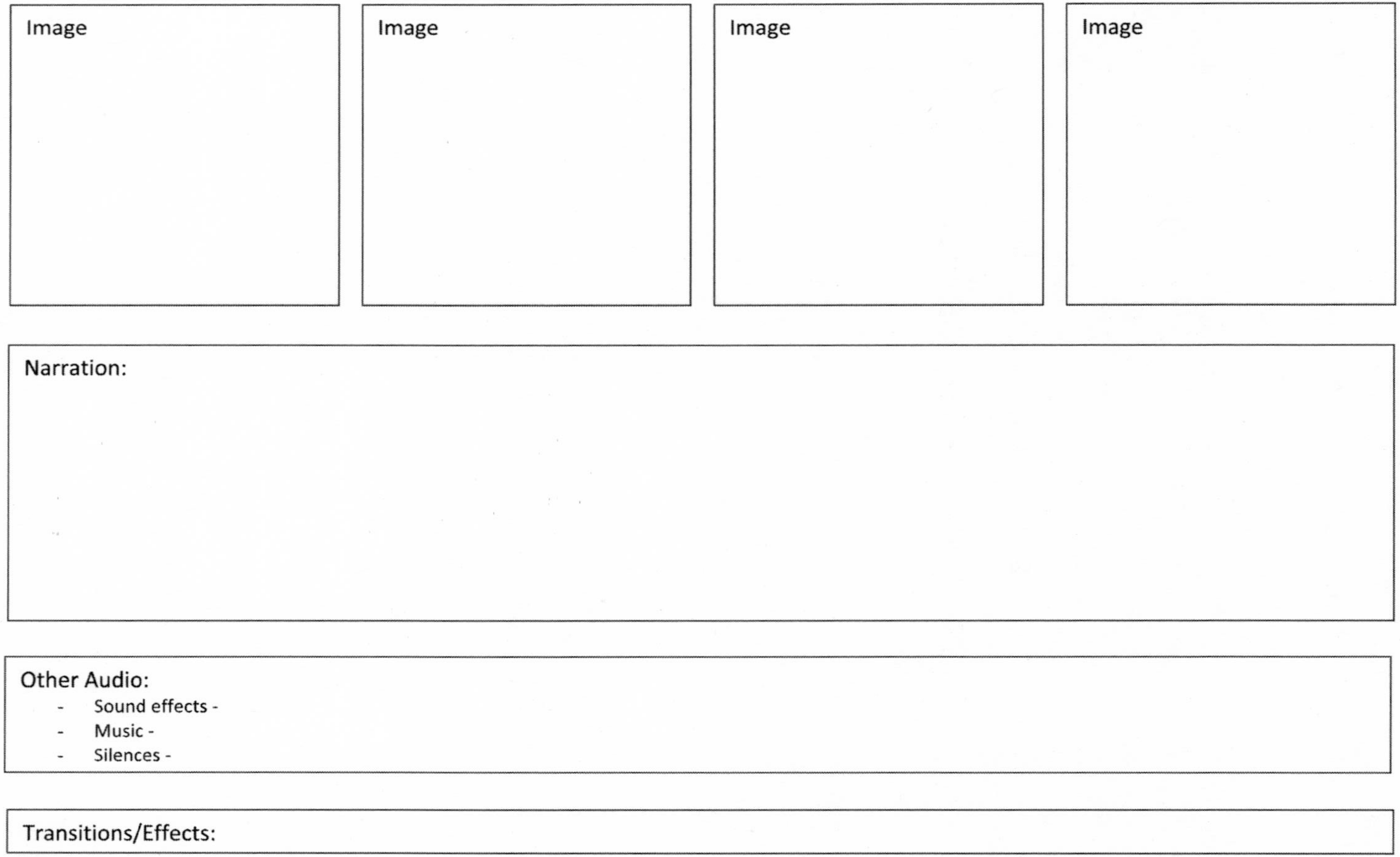

| Image | Image | Image | Image |

Narration:

Other Audio:
- Sound effects -
- Music -
- Silences -

Transitions/Effects:

Figure F1.1.

APPENDIX G
Software-Based Video Editors

Title	Tutorial QR Link	Platform	Cost	Features	Limitations
Apple Final Cut		Apple	$299.99	☑ Still Images ☑ Video Clips ☑ Transitions/Effects ☑ Separate Audio Track ☑ Audio Recording ☑ Audio Editing ☑ Export Options	• More complex program • File will corrupt if not saved properly
iMovie		Apple	$14.99	☑ Still Images ☑ Video Clips ☑ Transitions/Effects ☑ Separate Audio Track ☑ Audio Recording ☑ Audio Editing ☑ Export Options	• Movies with complex effects need to be shorter in length • Must work on the same computer for the entire project • Once exported, the movie can no longer be edited
Movie Maker		Windows	Free download with install of Windows	☑ Still Images ☑ Video Clips ☑ Transitions/Effects ☑ Separate Audio Track ☑ Audio Recording ☑ Audio Editing ☑ Export Options	• Movies with complex effects need to be shorter in length • Must work on the same computer for the entire project • Once exported, the movie can no longer be edited
Movie Plus		Serif Software	Free Download Or $79.99 for Full Package	☑ Still Images ☑ Video Clips ☑ Transitions/Effects ☑ Separate Audio Track ☑ Audio Recording ☑ Audio Editing ☑ Export Options	• Not available for Macs
Photo Story		Windows	Free download with install of Windows	☑ Still Images ☑ Video Clips ☑ Transitions/Effects ☑ Separate Audio Track ☑ Audio Recording ☑ Audio Editing ☑ Export Options	• Maximum number of images that may be imported in a single batch is 200 • Maximum output resolution is 1024 x 768 • Only supported video output format is .wmv • The crop and zoom tool is fixed at 4:3 aspect ratio • Not officially supported on Vista or Windows 7 platform, though will download and install

Figure G1.1a.

Pixorial		Web Tool (http://www.pixorial.com/)	**Free** for Educators **Premium**: varies	☑ Still Images ☑ Video Clips ☑ Transitions/Effects ☑ Separate Audio Track ☑ Audio Recording ☑ Audio Editing ☑ Export Options	• Does not convert all video formats • Requires Flash
Primary Access		Web Tool (http://www.primaryaccess.org/)	Free with account set-up	☑ Still Images ☐ Video Clips ☑ Transitions/Effects ☐ Separate Audio Track ☑ Audio Recording ☑ Audio Editing ☐ Export Options	• Must work within site • Only way to share movie is by sharing unique URL
Weavly		Web Tool (http://weavly.com/)	Free, No Download Required	☑ Still Images ☑ Video Clips ☐ Transitions/Effects ☑ Separate Audio Track ☐ Audio Recording ☑ Audio Editing ☐ Export Options	• Currently in Beta and only available with Flash
Wevideo		Web Tool (https://www.wevideo.com/)	**Lite:** Free **Plus:** $4.99/mo. $49.99/yr. **Ultra:** $9.99/mo. $99.99/yr.	☑ Still Images ☑ Video Clips ☑ Transitions/Effects ☑ Separate Audio Track ☑ Audio Recording ☑ Audio Editing ☑ Export Options	• Can take a long time to upload clips • No image stabilization, slow or fast motion • Requires Flash

Figure G1.1b.

APPENDIX H
Student Role Checklist

![Director icon] **Director**	☐ Oversees coordination of all roles insuring that each member completes individual and collective responsibilities. ☐ Takes the lead on communications with the teacher (e.g., film production updates). ☐ Takes responsibility for insuring that the interpretation developed during the research and storyboarding phases are not lost during the production phase. ☐ Organizes a screening of the Rough Cut film ☐ Collects and analyzes screening feedback and works with editor to incorporate suggestions. ☐ Exports the final video file and submits it to the teacher.

Figure H1.1.

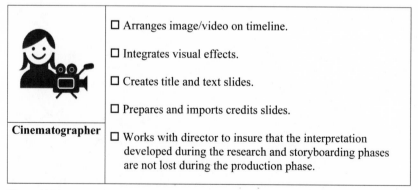

![Cinematographer icon] **Cinematographer**	☐ Arranges image/video on timeline. ☐ Integrates visual effects. ☐ Creates title and text slides. ☐ Prepares and imports credits slides. ☐ Works with director to insure that the interpretation developed during the research and storyboarding phases are not lost during the production phase.

Figure H1.2.

 **Talent**	☐ Responsible for narration of the film either as primary narrator or as coordinator of the narrating voices. ☐ Coordinates practice readings before recording for the film ☐ Provides peer feedback during rehearsals and recordings to improve delivery (e.g., inflection, emphasis). ☐ Matches tone of recording with the mood of the film. ☐ Organizes audio files for import.

Figure H1.3.   iStock photo

 **Audio Engineer**	☐ Imports audio narration files into appropriate places on the timeline. ☐ Works with director to develop audio effects (including silences) that help bring the interpretations developed during the research and storyboarding phases to life during the production phase. ☐ Integrates additional audio effects (e.g., fade in, fade out). ☐ Synchronizes music and other audio files on timeline. ☐ Works with cinematographer on timing of images and sound.

Figure H1.4.   iStock photo

 **Editor**	☐ Takes the lead on "micro edits" as the various pieces of the documentary come together. ☐ Work with the director to produce a Rough Cut of the film ☐ After the rough cut screening, and in consultation with the director, makes edits suggested by the audience and other production team members. ☐ Does the final work insuring that images, audio, and sounds are aligned according to the storyboard. ☐ Insure that the overall film has impact and is cohesive.

Figure H1.5.   iStock photo

INDEX